Successful SOCIAL NETWORKING in Public Libraries

WALT CRAWFORD

ala
editions

An imprint of the American Library Association
Chicago   2014

Walt Crawford is a writer, researcher, and sometimes speaker on libraries, technology, policy, and media. Recent research focuses on library use of social networks, but also on micro-publishing and library roles in that area. He has written 17 traditionally published books in the library field (and several self-published books), most recently *The Librarian's Guide to Micropublishing* (Information Today, Inc., 2012) and *Open Access: What You Need to Know Now* (ALA Editions, 2011). Crawford was a library systems analyst, designer, and programmer for five decades at RLG and the University of California and was president of LITA in 1992–1993. He received the LITA/Library Hi Tech Award for Outstanding Communication for Continuing Education in Library and Information Science in 1995, the ALCTS/Blackwell Scholarship Award (for *Future Libraries: Dreams, Madness & Reality*) in 1997, and the Gale Group Online Excellence in Information Authorship Award in 1998.

Printed in the United States of America

18 17 16 15 14   5 4 3 2 1

Extensive effort has gone into ensuring the reliability of the information in this book; however, the publisher makes no warranty, express or implied, with respect to the material contained herein.

ISBNs: 978-0-8389-1167-9 (paper); 978-0-8389-9611-9 (PDF). For more information on digital formats, visit the ALA Store at www.alastore.ala.org and select eEditions.

Library of Congress Cataloging-in-Publication Data
Crawford, Walt.
　　Successful social networking in public libraries / Walt Crawford.
　　　　pages　cm
　　Includes bibliographical references and index.
　　ISBN 978-0-8389-1167-9
　　1. Online social networks—Library applications.　I. Title.
　　Z674.75.S63C73 2014
　　302.30285—dc23

　　　　　　　　　　　　　　　　　　　　　　　　　　　　　　　　　　　　　2012036383

Book design by Casey Bayer in Andada and Din. Cover illustration © Shutterstock, Inc.

ALA Editions purchases fund advocacy, awareness, and accreditation programs
for library professionals worldwide.

♾ This paper meets the requirements of ANSI/NISO Z39.48–1992 (Permanence of Paper).

Contents

Preface

THIS BOOK HAS been a voyage of discovery—one that began with a loose agenda and ended with a greater appreciation for the sheer diversity of America's public libraries and the extent to which small libraries are the centers of their communities.

The loose agenda was not a set of theses and prescriptions for what constitutes successful social networking and whether public libraries were doing it right. Instead, I set out to see what was happening: how prevalent library social networking actually is and whether it seems to be reaching an audience.

I assumed then (in early 2011 when I proposed the project to ALA Editions) that most public libraries with active Facebook pages or Twitter accounts probably considered those efforts to be successful. After all, they're not long-established services with significant budget lines, ones that require decision making to retire. They're newcomers with little or no dedicated budget, ones that should be balanced against other initiatives. If they're not working, libraries should and, I believe, would redirect the time spent on social networks to some other, more profitable endeavor. That may have happened in some cases.

In other words, I assumed that librarians are intelligent people who generally know what they're doing. I did *not* assume that there was one and only one proper way to use Facebook or Twitter. I certainly did not assume that a public library serving four million people should have the same kind of Facebook page as one serving 400.

I also disbelieved the occasional assertion that all or almost all public libraries already had Facebook pages. That struck me as implausible, but it also struck me as easy to investigate. If, say, 180 of the first 200 libraries I checked had Facebook or Twitter accounts, then unless that sample was biased, I was wrong.

The appendix includes some notes on how the usage survey began and how (and why) it grew. Suffice it to say that what began as a two-state project possibly including 300 reporting libraries wound up as a 38-state project including nearly 6,000 public libraries—and the larger the body of data, the less willing I was to claim that the results could be projected to the rest of the country.

· Diversity in Size and Approach ·

I've always believed that the sheer diversity of America's public libraries is a strength, as is local control of those libraries. At the same time, although I was aware that most of America's public libraries are relatively small, I've always been a patron of medium-sized and large public libraries.

In the course of viewing library websites, Facebook pages, and Twitter streams, I've become much more aware of how many small libraries there are—and how effectively some of those libraries serve their community. Most small libraries don't have Facebook pages and few have Twitter accounts, but some small libraries clearly reach a substantial portion of their community through social networks.

Just as libraries differ in size, they differ in how they use social networks. That's as it should be, I believe. This book includes several dozen examples of public library tweeting and Facebook updates showing a range of approaches.

As of fall 2011, it was reasonable to say that most public libraries (at least in 38 of the 50 states) had social network accounts—but also that most public libraries were not active on either Facebook or Twitter. I suspect the latter statement won't be true by the time this book is published, as the rate of adoption appears to exceed the rate at which libraries stop updating social network accounts or shut them down.

· Acknowledgments ·

Thanks first to Susan Mark, statistics librarian at the Wyoming State Library. She has her own list of Facebook-using Wyoming libraries—and it was a different list than my initial results. An e-mail exchange convinced me to revisit 1,500 of the first 2,406 libraries, using an expanded search technique and finding many more Facebook accounts.

Thanks also to Colorado's Library Research Service for making freely available its study of 689 public libraries and their use of web technologies (including social networks) in 2010.

Thanks to all those who responded to my questions about social network use in their libraries. That includes 10 comments provided on a background-only basis as well as the following people who allowed me to quote them (although in some cases I didn't have room to include part or all of their comments):

- Ellen Druda at Half Hollow Hills Community Library in New York; Alan Thibeault at the Winthrop Public Library & Museum in Massachusetts; Gwendolyn Vos at Sioux Center Public Library in Iowa; Janette McMahon at West Liberty Public Library in Iowa; Amber Mussman at Cedar Rapids Public Library in Iowa; Jan Kaiser at Des Moines Public Library in Iowa; Diane Sinclair at Williams Public Library in Iowa; Vicki Hibbert at Clive Public Library in Iowa.
- Donna Robertson at Christchurch City Libraries in New Zealand; Ann Foster at the Saskatoon Public Library in Saskatchewan, Canada; Jamie Williams at Ericson

Public Library in Iowa; Cheryl Heid at Johnston Public Library in Iowa; Valerie Marino at Sawer Free Library in Massachusetts; Karen Burkett-Pederson at Bondurant Community Library in Iowa; Michelle McLean at Casey-Cardinia Library Corporation in Victoria, Australia; Claudia Haines at Homer Public Library in Alaska.

- Darcia Grace at Nenana City Library in Alaska; Anita Falltrick at Benicia Public Library in California; Barbara Eales at Ventura County Library in California; Terzah Becker at Boulder Public Library in Colorado; Marie Spratlin Hasskarl at Burlington Public Library in Connecticut; Andrea Ingala at Windsor Public Library in Connecticut; Carrie Andrew at Norwood Public Library in Colorado; Mary Lukkarila at Cloquet Public Library in Minnesota; Lynn Schofield-Dahl at Boulder City Library District in Nevada.

- Kit Thompson at Pierce County Library System in Washington; Theresa Barnaby at Richland Public Library in Washington; Marjorie Dailey at Albany County Public Library in Wyoming; Christina Greenfield at Big Horn County Library in Wyoming; Isabel M. Hoy at Goshen County Library in Wyoming; Melinda Brazzale at Laramie County Library System in Wyoming; Susan Worthen at Lyman Branch Library, Uinta County, Wyoming; Debbie Iverson at Sheridan County Public Library System in Wyoming; Moreno Barros at the University of Rio de Janeiro in Brazil; David Bigwood at the Lunar and Planetary Institute in Texas.

- David Lee King of the Topeka and Shawnee County Library System in Kansas, who made a case for *not* having network icons on the library home page; the Library Society of the World contingent on FriendFeed for a variety of discussions; and others who helped bring this project about—including, last but most important, my patient and supportive wife (who has been a public library cataloging supervisor and an academic library director, albeit before library social networking was feasible).

This project involved a rolling snapshot of how 5,958 public libraries in 38 states use two social networks. I believe this book will be useful for every library that has a Facebook page or Twitter account—and for every library that's considering such activity.

CHAPTER 1

SOCIAL NETWORKING IN PUBLIC LIBRARIES

LIBRARIES SHOULD BE active within their communities and visible to their patrons.

That doesn't seem like a controversial statement. Here's one that might be a little more troublesome: Libraries should be where patrons *want* or *expect* them to be, when that's feasible and appropriate.

The flip side of that statement: Libraries should not intrude on the lives of their patrons when such intrusion is unwanted—and what's helpful at one level may become intrusive at another level.

This book considers public libraries in social networks—specifically, how public libraries were using Facebook and Twitter in the fall of 2011. These social networks offer new ways for libraries to be active within their communities and engage their patrons. Many libraries use Facebook effectively. Many others have Facebook pages but may not be effectively reaching and engaging their patrons. Thanks to the wonders of Facebook Community Pages, many public libraries also have Facebook pages that they did not create and may not be aware of.

Public library Twitter accounts are much less widespread, but there are still hundreds of them, almost certainly more than a thousand nationwide. Neither Facebook nor Twitter is a universal solution, and no single set of guidelines for their use will serve all libraries equally well. What I hope to do here is to show what's being done and offer a variety of examples of how libraries use these networks—and what some librarians and library workers have to say about that use. Along the way, I'll note a couple of ways that libraries can *fail* at social networking, with the caveat that there are many more ways to succeed than to fail.

Before diving into Facebook and Twitter, it may be useful to think a little more about library community activity and patron engagement in general. I believe there's a set of questions that should be considered (not necessarily answered) for any such activity—whether you call it marketing, outreach, engagement, or publicity.

· Not Only Whether, but Also Which and How ·

You may have read or heard that all or nearly all public libraries are already on Facebook. That is simply not true. At least as of fall 2011, there are thousands of U.S. public libraries that have neither library-maintained Facebook pages nor Twitter accounts.

Does every library *need* to be on Facebook? Clearly not, although library social networking gurus have made such suggestions. After years of hearing "every library must . . ." and "every librarian should . . ." followed by various things that couldn't possibly apply to every library, I think a reasonable filter is to place before the "should" or "must" this qualifier: ". . . that has at least the resources of libraries I'm most familiar with." So, for example, according to Angel Rivera's notes on David Lee King's November 2011 webinar on "Facebook in the Library: Enhancing Library Services and Engaging Users," King said: "Libraries need to be in Facebook given that our communities are there already."[1] As a general proposition, saying that libraries need to be wherever their communities are is absurd, but *within context*—including, most important, that *these* librarians all had resources and time to attend a webinar—King may be right. (Incidentally, Rivera's post outlines a number of good suggestions from King on goals and techniques for Facebook.)

Are most U.S. public libraries already on Facebook or Twitter? That's not clear. In a summer 2011 survey of public library agencies in 25 states, slightly less than half (48%) appeared to have either library-run Facebook pages or Twitter accounts. The missing majority was not just smaller rural libraries, however. Although a majority of libraries serving 25,000 people or more *did* have Facebook pages, more than a third of those libraries were not apparently active on Facebook or Twitter.

A majority of libraries in 38 states *did* have either library-run Facebook pages or Twitter accounts when checked in fall 2011, including a majority of libraries in the original 25 states, but in both cases it was a narrow majority: 54% of the 2,406 public libraries in 25 states and 55% of 5,958 libraries in 38 states. That's with the broadest possible definition of "have," including pages that have never had posts and pages and Twitter accounts with no posts or tweets in more than a year. That still leaves 45% of public libraries checked—just under 2,700—with no apparent social network presence. Indeed, the majority is so small that I would *not* be willing to assert that a majority of all public libraries in all 50 states have social network presences. It's quite possible that participation within the remaining 12 states (involving more than 3,000 more libraries, most of them small) was low enough to reduce overall involvement to less than half.

SHOULD YOUR LIBRARY BE ON SOCIAL NETWORKS?

Answering that question involves some thought and a little planning—and maybe a little research. Let's break it down into several smaller questions that need to be answered for each social network you may be considering:

- *Can your library devote staff time to create and manage the social network account?* For some smaller libraries, "staff" includes (or may consist entirely of) volunteers, but this question needs to be answered in every case. A social network presence that's empty may be worse than no social network presence at all. A social network presence with nobody assigned primary responsibility might as well not exist.

Opening an account on a social network is free. Maintaining an effective account most definitely is not, although the cost is staff time, not money.

- *Can your library sustain activity on this social network, not only posting items but also following up on feedback?* I'm not ready to say your library should post something every day (that's ludicrous for many libraries) but if you're successful, someone should be checking your account every day the library is open and probably at least once every open hour during that time. You also need to have some plan for succession and backup so that social network activity doesn't cease abruptly when one person leaves or is out of the library for an extended period.

- *Does your community use this social network?* At this point, the answer is likely to be yes for Facebook. For Twitter, the answer is less clear in some communities.

- *Do your patrons expect or want to see you on this network?* Your goal should be to increase community involvement, engagement with, and support of the library—not to be an intrusion into areas where patrons don't think the library belongs. Is your library ready to treat this social network as what it is—that is, a social network? Ideally, social networks involve engagement. Your library should be listening to your community and engaging with it. You should be talking with your patrons, not just to them.

That last question moves from *whether* to *how*. If there's one thing I'm sure of after glancing at how more than 3,200 libraries use Facebook and how more than 950 use Twitter, it's that no set of rules applies to everybody. There is no doubt that some libraries use Facebook or Twitter strictly as another publicity medium, *to good effect* and with good results. Is it the best use of either network, however? I don't believe it is, but I'm not willing to claim that as unassailable truth.

WHICH NETWORKS?

With all its failings and privacy issues, Facebook is currently the more than 1.1-billion-user whale in the social networking ocean. Given Facebook's claim that half its users check in at least once a day, that's particularly impressive. That 1.1 billion figure is worldwide. U.S. and Canadian usage may be falling, but you can still assume that roughly half of your patrons have Facebook accounts—and that roughly one-quarter of them use those accounts every day.

You could make the claim that Facebook's shoddy and ever-changing privacy practices make it a poor match for libraries, but that's a discussion beyond the scope of this book. In practice, Facebook suits libraries because it has pages designed for organizations and companies, so people can follow you by "liking" your page rather than by the clumsy reciprocal "friending" formerly required for personal accounts. (That has changed, however; people can now follow other people's feeds on Facebook without requiring reciprocity.)

After Facebook, there's a huge drop in usage. According to comScore's December 2012 rankings by unique visitors from U.S. addresses, Facebook had 150 million U.S. visitors (a drop from 162 million in August 2011). [2] Twitter was a distant second at 40.7 million (up from 33 million in August 2011). LinkedIn was nearly tied for second at 40.6 million. MySpace, which was second with 37 million in August 2011, was number 48 at 27.5 million.

At this point, MySpace appears to focus primarily on entertainment and music. It's also gained a reputation for some less savory pages and lost much of its usage within the United States. In my initial scan of 2,406 public library websites in 25 states in the summer of 2011,

I found 21 libraries with MySpace icons on their home pages—and I'd have to wonder how many of those were active sites.

The obvious second choice for library involvement is Twitter, and hundreds of public libraries use Twitter. Like Facebook, Twitter doesn't require reciprocity: any number of people can follow your library's tweets without your approval. But it's much less widely used than Facebook; as noted earlier, it has roughly one-quarter the usage. Given the probability that Twitter users aren't spread as evenly across the population as Facebook appears to be, it's more than possible that, in many smaller communities, there aren't enough Twitter users to make a library account worthwhile. There are other factors to Twitter usage as well—for example, crafting messages within the 140-character limit that aren't just links and maintaining the level of activity that seems to be expected of tweeters.

Then there's LinkedIn. To most of us, it's a business network, primarily for business and professional relationships. It makes sense for a library to use LinkedIn as one recruiting tool. Does it make sense to use it as part of social networking? I've seen some libraries on LinkedIn, but I believe it's an open question as to whether this network is where patrons *expect* or *want* to interact with libraries.

Among 3,266 public libraries with a social network presence in fall 2011, 57—6% of the libraries using Twitter—appeared to use *only* Twitter. That is, they didn't have visible Facebook accounts other than teen or children's pages. I can only assume that in these five dozen cases librarians made a conscious decision that *for their community and patrons* Twitter was a better network.

Google+ began offering pages for organizations in late fall 2011. Before then, it was not feasible for public libraries to maintain a Google+ presence, at least not legitimately. When I was rechecking the 2,406 libraries in 25 states, I observed perhaps half a dozen G+ icons leading to Google+ pages. It's fair to assume that there will be many more Google+ library pages in the future—if Google+ grows to be a serious alternative to Facebook.

· Communities and Social Networks ·

It really is all about community and engagement—or at least it can be. An effective social network presence can combine functions of a bulletin board where patrons post questions or complaints and staff members post responses, library blogs, the news area of your website, and your e-mailed newsletter. That presence can have a single focus, but more often it will include a range of topics and even voices.

But every community is different, just as every library is different. At one extreme, two libraries in Alaska, one in New Mexico, and one in Idaho, each serving fewer than 300 people, have Facebook pages liked by roughly half the people in the community—a level that's unheard of for larger libraries. (Among the 5,958 libraries in this study, the highest percentage of Facebook likes for libraries serving at least 25,000 people was just over 7% of the community; for libraries serving at least 500,000, it was 2.6%.)

Should the Los Angeles Public Library (LAPL), serving just over four million people, or the County of Los Angeles Public Library (serving more than 3.6 million) be unhappy because they don't have two million likes? Clearly not. For that matter, should the updates from LAPL and other huge public libraries sound the same or serve the same purposes as those from Hope Community Library, the Village of Corona Public Library, Stanley District Library, and Seldovia Public Library?

Consider some Facebook updates from four very small public libraries. Here's Hope Community Library in Alaska with feedback noted by boldface first names, last names omitted:

> All—I had hoped to post more about the Hope Wagon Run that will be this weekend; however, I have been unable to get any electronic information to pass along. The Wagon Run will be this Sunday and there will be lots of events throughout the weekend in Hope. **3 people like this.**
>
> **Breezy** Looking forward to it! We'll be headed that way in the morning!
>
> **Susan** Pancake breakfast from 8–11am at the social hall, cake walk at 3pm, music at the seaview, antique car parades through the day, and Sunday is the Run at 11am. Raffle will start at 2pm.

> Wow, summer is in full swing and it is looking fabulous outside! Check out our book shed for an inexpensive book to stick in your back pocket. Then, go find that perfect spot off the beaten path and spend some time living in someone else's imagination. **5 people like this.**

That first post is *direct* engagement: The library filled in the basics and a community member added the particulars. Seldovia Public Library, also in Alaska, weighs in with a slightly more formal tone:

> Board meeting: Tuesday, August 8 at 7pm Agenda Annual meeting of the Seldovia Public Library Board of Directors August 9, 2011 at 7 pm Roll call (excused absences) Call to order . . .

> The Big Bang: How do they know that? Seldovians for Science and the Seldovia Public Library invite you to Dr. Travis Rector An evening with Dr. Travis Rector Dr. Rector is a professor of physics and astronomy at the University of Alaska Anchorage. . . .

> Look for us on the Fourth! That's right: we'll be there for our annual used book sale, just as we are every year: library parking lot starting at 7 am. And oh, have we got some great books for you this year. We did a big weeding of our fiction section last year and there are bunches of novels by your favorite authors. . . .

Here's a third, very small library, Stanley District Library in Idaho:

> The library will be closed tomorrow. Stop by our booth at the Sawtooth Mountain Mamas Arts and Crafts Fair to purchase your 2012 calendar. **Chris likes this.**

Buy the 2012 Sawtooth Scenes Calendar, Now Available Online! [Link]

It was a big snow year in the Sawtooths and while the flakes flew outside our team of volunteers was poring through photographs and looking at proofs. The result is a gorgeous calendar showcasing the beauty that surrounds us here in Stanley, Idaho. It may be the best of our calendars yet. As always. **2 people like this.**

Stanley Community Library created an event. Third annual Friends of the Library Luncheon Friday, July 29, 2011 at 12:00pm Redfish Lake Lodge

Songwriter Josh Ritter from Moscow, Idaho has published his first book, "Bright's Passage." Check it out!

    Heather Awesome. I love his music!

And here's the Village of Corona Public Library in New Mexico—with four updates over an eight-day period in November in a library potentially serving 185 people (with 100 Facebook likes):

LAST CHANCE to get your important dates, ads and brands into the 2012 Corona Community Calendar! The calendar goes to the printer on November 16. All proceeds benefit the library and literacy in the Corona area. Pick up a form at the library or email us at friends_of_vocpl@ yahoo.com to get your order form. Thank you!

NM Centennial Steam Train passes through Corona on Saturday, Nov 11. (Photo courtesy of Alvina H.) **5 people like this.**

    Trish Phenomenal Photo!!

    Great picture Alvina

GREAT NEWS!! The Library has just received many new Non-fiction DVDs which are now ready to check out! Subjects include animals, sports (rodeo, basketball, football), places (Rift Valley, Ganges, Yellowstone, the Universe), people (the Apostles, the Founding Fathers, cowboys), music (Elvis, Taylor Swift, Cats the musical), events (Mayflower crossing, 9/11/01, and comedy (Gilda Radner, Steve Martin) just to name a few. COME BY AND SEE IT FOR YOURSELF!! **2 people like this.**

IT'S THAT TIME AGAIN, FOLKS!!! The Friends of the Village of Corona Public Library are now taking orders for the 2012 Corona Community Calendar! The price is still an easy $10. If you have any questions, please call the Library or any member of the Friends of VOCPL and they will be glad to help. CALL OR COME BY NOW!!

Heather I want a calendar . . . but it would take me too long to come by the library. Can I mail a check? :)

Village of Corona Public Library We will mail you an order form tomorrow!!

Susan I would like a calendar as well. I live in Arizona so could it be mailed to me?

Village of Corona Public Library Absolutely, Susan! We will contact you with info!!

Each of these four libraries, primarily if not entirely volunteer-run, serves fewer than 300 people. At the other extreme, here's LAPL, serving more than four *million* people—and it's worth noting that LAPL's updates also maintain a personal voice (one post has been trimmed):

Who knew our Chatsworth Branch Library was a hotbed of young, cutting-edge musical talent? Check out Patch Magazine's video coverage of the August 18th Teen Concert event at the branch. **[Video] 3 people like this.**

LA City = Books R Us! Is L.A. The World's Next Great Literary City? The Los Angeles Review of Books Says Yes: **[Link]** That's right: the days of dogging LA book culture might soon (finally!) be behind us thanks to The Los Angeles Review of Books, an ambitious new LA-based literature review journal that's re-imagining the art of literary critique and propelling it into the 21st century. Digital, sprawling, and fearless . . . **6 people like this.**

Those are extremes: some of the smallest and largest libraries among Facebook users in the 25 states surveyed. You'll find more personal but also more formal attitudes in between.

I believe all five libraries serve their communities well and engage them effectively with Facebook, albeit at different levels of engagement. (LAPL has more than 3,000 likes—but that's less than one per thousand residents, typical of very large libraries.)

HOW SMALL?

The Alaska, New Mexico, and Idaho libraries noted earlier are *not* the smallest libraries in the 38 states surveyed—not even the smallest with Facebook pages. There are 27 libraries serving fewer than 100 people. One of those established a Facebook page in the late summer of 2011. Here are three Facebook updates of four over the course of 16 days from Whale Pass Community Library—with nine likes in a legal service area of *31 people:*

> Winter hours are in effect now: Monday 3–5 pm Tuesday 1–3 pm Wednesday 4–8 pm Saturday 11 am–2 pm WIFI available indoors and out—electrical outlets on the side deck with table and chairs.

> Big winds yesterday—all the notices on the bulletin board flew away— lots of room for new posts now.

> We just had our first story time for and with the children from Whale Pass School—what fun! Thursday mornings will be something to look forward to in the coming weeks. Next week, we'll take pictures!

I omitted a September 22 post with six new photos from that second reading day. It's worth noting that there *are* posts from others on the wall: the library is engaging the community.

Sometimes, not all of the likes for a public library Facebook page are from members of the local community. One small library in New Mexico has a legal service area of 439 and 755 likes on its Facebook account; clearly, those aren't all patron likes. Still, when I've checked Facebook likes and Twitter follows (where it's possible to do so), all but a few apparently have been either patrons, local businesses, and organizations or fans of the library from nearby communities. Yes, some librarians like or follow a fair number of libraries around the country—but that doesn't appear to be a substantial portion of any library's following.

IS ENGAGEMENT MANDATORY?

Is it wrong for a library to use Facebook or Twitter purely as a publication channel with no room for actual engagement? I'm not ready to make that claim. Anita Falltrick, technology librarian at Benicia Public Library in California (serving 28,000 people, with an average of 10 to 15 tweets and Facebook updates per month) had this to say:

> We use both as another form of outreach mostly for events. The center section of our website's homepage is a blog. Each week I either copy and paste or link each blog story from our homepage to Facebook and then I shorten the entry to fit in Twitter. We have linked the events page to our Google calendar. *We do not allow comments with either of these social media. It's another way to reach out to people who do not use our website or paper calendars.* [Emphasis added]

With 87 followers and 154 likes as of late November 2011 (up from 67 and 131 in late August) and a streamlined workflow, social networks may be an effective way to reach out—even without comments. Notably, Falltrick *does* create shorter tweets, rather than simply offering the first portion of a Facebook update and a link. Here are two tweets from Benicia followed by the equivalent Facebook updates:

Teen Karaoke Party—Wed, Jul 27, 6–8 pm. What better way to spend a summer night than with your friends, some karaoke and treats?

Poetry Reading—Thurs, July 28, 7 pm. Poems written for the exhibit "I Read the News Today, Oh Boy!" will be read by their writers.

Teen Karaoke Party | Benicia Public Library. **[Link]** What better way to spend a summer night than with your friends and some karaoke? Join us at the library for some tunes and some tantalizing treats to wet your whistle in between songs! **Janet likes this.**

I Read the News Today, Oh Boy! Poetry Reading | Benicia Public Library. **[Link]** Poems created for the exhibit will be read as well as related work by distinguished poets who participated in the project.

Janette McMahon, director of the West Liberty Public Library in Iowa—serving 3,300 people with 153 likes in September 2011 and fairly frequent posts (around three per week in recent months)—also sees Facebook as primarily a one-way tool: "West Liberty Public Library uses Facebook for promotion and dissemination of information. We do not use Twitter."

But even a quick glance at West Liberty's Facebook wall shows that "promotion and dissemination" does not mean impersonal or lifeless posts:

Make sure you save us a little time right after trick-or-treating Halloween night. More info to come bwahahaha . . . **2 people like this.**

Whew, just finished updating the Library events. We've got A LOT going on this month!

West Liberty Public Library created an event. Wimpy Kid Lock-In Friday, September 30, 2011 at 8:00pm West Liberty Public Library RSVP to this event . . . [followed by more event posts].

On the other hand, engagement *is* an important part of social networking for many libraries and can go hand-in-hand with understanding your community. Terza Becker, reference librarian at the Boulder Public Library (Colorado), serving 97,000 people with *very* active Twitter and Facebook accounts—averaging more than one tweet and update per day, and with more than 950 likes and 1,380 followers—and following more than 1,500 people, offers this commentary:

Boulder is a tech-savvy college town (home to the giant University of Colorado, several federal labs and numerous venture capitalist firms and technology start-ups), so *meeting them in the places they frequent (many of which are now virtual) is mandatory for us.*

We've had our Facebook page and Twitter accounts for a couple of years. For a while, we didn't get a lot of fans/followers or traffic. But it's been really picking up this year thanks in part to the facts that we have a dynamic new Web master and that two of our reference librarians (one of whom is me!) had our jobs redefined to *specifically* include an emphasis on bridging the communication gap between the digital side of the library and the public-facing desk side.

Our most successful posts are the ones that invite people to interact with us (questions, RA type things where we suggest books to people via Facebook, funny things, anecdotes about our building and our colorful patrons, pictures of Boulder Creek which runs right below our building). [Emphasis added]

Boulder's tweets do seem to be the first few words of the Facebook posts, followed by links to those posts. Here are three posts (edited for length) from a one-week period in August 2011 showing some of the range of Boulder's approach—and some of the feedback that resulted:

A little humor for your day. . . . Yeah, Kindles will complicate things like book burnings. . . . **[Link] 7 people like this.**

> **Todd** Heh. :-)

A young girl came to the children's desk and said, "I found the books on cats, but I can't find the books on cheetahs." I responded, "Cats are in the pet section, let me show you where the wild animal section is. I'm assuming you don't want a cheetah for a pet right?" She replied, "Well, I keep asking my mom and she says no, but I am going to learn how to take care of cheetahs and then maybe she will let me have one for a pet." **23 people like this.**

> **Manifestor** Cheetah power animal!

> **Timothy** little cutie

Books can change your life or at least shift your points of view. For this librarian, two that come to mind are Peter Hessler's *River Town* and Toni Morrison's *Jazz*. What about you? What book affected you deeply and why? The Happiness Project: 7 Books That Changed the Way I See the World. **[Link]**

Casey Reading James Salter's LIGHT YEARS feels like taking vitamins for the soul and mind. Evidence seems to appear in my own writing, and I find more light in my view.

Joanne "Perfection of the Morning: A Woman's Awakening in Nature" by Sharon Butala. It led to a new way of seeing our connection with the natural world as well as women's place in that world. I recommend the book to everyone.

Community engagement is at the heart of many libraries' use of social networks, but—as with most expectations—it's not a universal need. For some libraries in some communities, a new broadcast channel may be what's feasible and what's needed.

· Some Definitions and Caveats ·

This book is based on an external survey of all the public libraries or library systems I could locate in 38 of the 50 United States—5,958 in all, or just under two-thirds of the 9,184 public libraries in the United States. More details on the stages of the survey appear in the appendix. It's also based on direct comments from several dozen librarians on their own use of social networks, notably including more than a dozen libraries that are *not* within the 38 states (three of them are outside the United States entirely).

While there are a lot of numbers in this book, it's mostly about the libraries and what they're doing. So that I don't need to repeat "probably" and "roughly" and "at least" and various other qualifiers too often, you should be aware of some definitions, simplifications, and caveats up front. Definitions also include a new grouping of public libraries by size that I find useful in discussing public libraries in social networks.

In many cases, general terms will be used in this book as follows:

Public library: A library or library system that has a defined legal service area (LSA) population and reports to its state library and/or the Institute for Museum and Library Services (IMLS). That does not include branch libraries. It does, in some cases, include double-counting in states where library systems and individual libraries within those systems both have LSAs and both report.

LSA: Legal service area population as given in the most recent spreadsheet available from state libraries (as downloaded in July 2011 for 25 libraries and late August 2011 for 13 others). In most discussions, I round the LSA to the nearest thousand (the nearest hundred or 10 for small libraries).

Page: Sometimes used for both Facebook pages and Twitter accounts, noting that Facebook pages also include a few regular Facebook accounts (with friends rather than likes) and a few Facebook groups.

Likes: I usually use "likes" for the number of friends or likes or group members on a Facebook page or account, although "fans" is the more common usage. If I use fans it may refer to both Facebook likes and Twitter followers.

HAPLR size or H#: Ten divisions of public libraries by LSA, as used in Hennen's American Public Library Ratings. The divisions are noted in the appendix. I sometimes use H# for a brief version of HAPLR sizes—from 0 (libraries serving fewer than 1,000 people) to 9 (libraries serving 500,000 or more).

Urban and rural: A two-way split of libraries by size, with "urban" indicating libraries potentially serving at least 25,000 people (H5–9) and "rural" indicating libraries potentially serving fewer than 25,000 people (H0–4). I find this split too broad, just as I find it silly to call Darien, Connecticut, "rural."

Small, medium, and large: My own attempt at a slightly more useful split of libraries by size. Small libraries are those potentially serving fewer than 10,000 people (H0–3); medium libraries are those potentially serving 10,000 to 99,999 people (H4–6); large libraries are those potentially serving 100,000 or more (H7–9).

Presence: I define Facebook presence as broadly as reasonably possible, including accounts with no updates or no likes and those that haven't been updated in more than a year—but excluding Community Pages (with no apparent library involvement), cases where libraries had teen or children's Facebook pages but not general-purpose pages, and pages I couldn't find using the methods detailed in the appendix. Twitter presence includes all Twitter accounts I could find, including those with no tweets and those that haven't had a tweet in more than a year.

Activity: It's reasonable to look at numbers of posts or tweets as one aspect of social network presence and success. Chapter 2 includes the definition of one breakdown of both currency and frequency in six levels from very frequent (five or more posts within the week checked) to moribund (no posts within the last quarter). That six-way breakdown (numbers 1–6) is used later in the book as well.

Reach: After looking at the reality of Facebook pages and Twitter accounts, I've defined a five-level breakdown for reach that partially depends on the library's LSA population, using the small, medium, or large split. Chapter 2 includes the definition of that breakdown from broad reach (10% or more of the LSA for small libraries, 1,000 or more likes or followers for medium libraries, and 3,000 or more for large libraries) to minimal reach (usually indicating a very new account or one that's essentially dead: less than 1% of LSA for small libraries, fewer than 100 likes for medium libraries, and fewer than 300 for large libraries).

There are three obvious and important caveats to these general terms:

- I surveyed only 5,958 libraries in 38 states, leaving out more than 3,000 libraries in 12 states. Given how much states differ in character, I am not willing to project the figures for these 38 states and 5,958 libraries to all 50 states and 9,000-plus libraries. There's a little more on that in the appendix.
- I could measure only what I found. The appendix details the process I used. It's nearly certain that I missed a few well-hidden Facebook pages and Twitter accounts, just as I may have missed a few library websites entirely. I *know* that the pages and accounts discussed here exist (or existed when I checked them); I have not verified that others do not, although I'd guess there are very few of them.
- Your library—that is, the librarians and staff of your library—is the only agency that can determine whether or not your social networking is successful and what defines success. I can offer benchmarks, criteria, and numbers showing actual practice, but those benchmarks and criteria aren't rules.

·The Rest of This Book·

The rest of this book expands and fleshes out the numbers and offers a range of examples of Facebook and Twitter strategies—and how the two relate. I spend more time on community involvement and note some problems with social networks.

The last part of the book considers change. I rechecked the libraries in 25 states originally checked in late July through late August 2011 four months later to see how many have added Facebook or Twitter accounts and updated the level of activity and likes/followers for library accounts.

You'll see lots of examples throughout the book and a few dozen more comments, both signed comments and paraphrased comments provided on a background-only basis. This book is about how and why public libraries use social networks. I'm hoping it will help you and your library to see how you compare to others, to see what others are doing, and to consider what you might change to make social networking more effective in your library and your community.

A NOTE ON SOURCES

Most of the quoted material in this book comes either from tweets and status updates or from several dozen e-mailed responses to some questions that I posed on my blog and on several library lists. I am not footnoting those sources. For tweets and updates, they're either identified along with the quoted material or, in some cases, anonymized (since I have no interest in making libraries look bad). I have deleted last names in user feedback within tweets and updates. For other quotations (and background comments) that do *not* have citations, consider this to be the universal citation: Personal e-mail to me, sometime in July–September 2011. I'm grateful to all those who responded, including 10 who preferred that I not quote them directly. The acknowledgments include other respondents.

Tweets and Facebook updates were copied directly from Facebook walls and Twitter pages. In many cases, they have been edited for length and to simplify formatting. Some minor typos have been corrected as well. Where feedback appears (other than likes), it's broken to the next line with the person's name (omitting last name) in boldface. URLs are replaced with **[Link]**, and most text that appears to come from such URLs is omitted.

A FEW WORDS ON LAURA SOLOMON'S
DOING SOCIAL MEDIA SO IT MATTERS

Laura Solomon wrote *Doing Social Media So It Matters*, published as an ALA Editions Special Report in 2011, based partly on her own experience using social networks to try to save Ohio's public libraries from a threatened massive cut in state funding.

In some ways, this book follows up on Solomon's work—but with substantial differences. Solomon has been a public library web supervisor; I've never worked in a public library. Solomon has strong opinions as to what works and what doesn't; I'm looking at how libraries across the country (and in a few cases around the world) are using social networks, offering a range of existing models with few strong opinions of my own.

To take the most extreme difference in treatment, Solomon says this on lack of content as a reason for social media failure:

> Your library needs to post very regularly. If your social media posts only happen
> a couple of times per week, this is not enough to build on, especially in a medium
> where twenty-four hours is an exceptionally long amount of time to go without
> any communication. Ensure you're participating daily at the absolute minimum.[3]

If "participating" means posting or tweeting, that makes most public library social networking failures. Among Facebook pages, based on the five most recent posts when checked, only one-fifth of Facebook pages and one-third of Twitter accounts averaged five posts a week (or roughly one a day). I'm unwilling to assert that four out of five libraries with Facebook pages and two out of three libraries with Twitter accounts are failing. For any library serving fewer than 10,000 patrons, I'll say that a post a day is extraordinary activity (although some small libraries do seem to meet that criterion).

Similarly, Solomon says that libraries using Twitter should follow about as many people as follow the library—a criterion that says half of library Twitter users are doing it wrong.

Laura Solomon's book is well worth reading. Maybe her stiffer criteria for success make sense. Those criteria are not applied in this book; I just can't write off so many libraries. At the same time, Solomon offers so much good advice on a range of social networking issues that I encourage you to buy her book and read it carefully.

NOTES

1. Angel Rivera, "Webinar Notes: David Lee King on 'Facebook in the Library,'" *The Gypsy Librarian*, January 4, 2012, http://gypsylibrarian.blogspot.com/2012/01/webinar-notes-david-lee-king-on.html.

2. comScore, Inc., "comScore Media Metrix Ranks Top 50 U.S. Web Properties for December 2012," press release, January 28, 2013, www.comscore.com/content/download/18905/900893/file/comScore%20Media%20Metrix%20Ranks%20Top%2050%20U.S.%20Web%20Properties%20for%20December%202012.pdf.

3. Laura Solomon, *Doing Social Media So It Matters: A Librarian's Guide* (Chicago: American Library Association, 2011), 53.

CHAPTER 2

WHAT CONSTITUTES SUCCESS IN YOUR LIBRARY?

ARE YOUR PUBLIC library's social networking efforts successful? Probably. The efforts probably aren't as successful as they could be, but they're probably successful.

I'm making an optimistic assumption here that I believe is warranted, given that public library social networking efforts aren't the old, entrenched services that can't be gotten rid of. With the exception of MySpace, social networks haven't been around long enough, at a scale where public libraries would plausibly participate, for them to be truly entrenched services.

Given their relative youth and that they compete for time and attention with other initiatives, it's fair to assume most public libraries wouldn't maintain active Facebook pages or Twitter accounts unless they were reasonably satisfied with the results.

· It's Working If You Think It Is ·

This statement presents the essential value proposition for public library social networking and for most other library initiatives that don't involve significant capital investment or space usage that can't readily be reassigned.

If you're getting 1% more attendance at your programs and you're pretty sure that correlates to the time spent posting and tweeting, that may be good enough.

If you've been able to notify 2% or 200 of your patrons about a library emergency or a community emergency, that may represent a benefit many times as great as the time required to start your Twitter and Facebook accounts and the trivial time required to post items about the emergency.

If one out of 10 Facebook updates gets a comment from a patron, a comment suggesting stronger support of the library, you may find that justification enough for the entire effort—

especially when you *respond* to the comment, helping to turn a casual patron into a stronger library advocate.

If your friends group gains 10 new members or sells 100 more "gently used" books as a result of your activity in social networks, that's probably reward enough.

In these and many other ways, your library's social networking can be successful *by your standards,* regardless of what other libraries are doing.

So you can skip the rest of the book, right?

If you're a public librarian and *entirely* satisfied with your library's Facebook and Twitter efforts, I doubt that you've made it this far unless you're interested in the broader picture (as I hope you are). Otherwise, you're probably in at least one of these real-world categories:

- Your library is one of the 45% that isn't on Facebook or Twitter—or, more likely, one of the roughly 85% that isn't on Twitter. In either case, you're wondering whether you should be.
- Your library doesn't seem to be reaching many people, or at least not as many as you hoped.
- Your library's tweets and updates don't yield much feedback.
- The people doing the tweets or updates wonder whether their time is well spent.
- You wonder whether your Facebook page and Twitter account are beneficial to the library's public image.
- You're finding internal controversy over what should and should not be posted—and the appropriate tone for posts and tweets.

I can't offer direct answers. This book can help in several regards. You'll find broad statistical analyses and specific library examples in your peer categories—peer by size and by state—that may help you evaluate your own efforts. You'll see examples of actual usage. And you'll see a range of suggestions from me and from librarians that you may find helpful.

CHANCES ARE, IT COULD BE BETTER: THE 80/20 RULE

Here's the flip side of the basic assertion that it's working if you think it is: Chances are your social networking could be *more* successful than it is.

There's a rough metric that applies in many situations involving large, heterogeneous groups. It's a variant of the 80/20 rule. Here's how I'd state it in terms of library social network presence: Among libraries that are on Facebook or Twitter, roughly one-fifth are likely to be *very* successful, roughly one-fifth are likely to be struggling, and roughly three-fifths are likely to be successful but not as successful as they'd like to be. In other words, roughly four-fifths of library social networking efforts could plausibly be more successful than they are, without such an extraordinary effort that it would make the process unsupportable.

You could argue with the limit points (some would use one-quarter and one-half, some extremists might use one-tenth for the "very successful" group and as much as three-tenths or four-tenths for the "struggling or unsuccessful" group), but the 80/20 rule of thumb works well in a remarkably varied set of circumstances.

Before looking at some 80/20 points, let's consider some metrics.

· Frequency, Currency, and Reach ·

Two external measures of Facebook pages and Twitter accounts are frequency and reach. I think it makes sense to consider currency as part of frequency.

Frequency is the rate at which updates or tweets appear. An incredibly high-frequency Facebook account might have 10 updates a day. While I don't know of any library pages that are quite *that* active, there are 41 that, at least at one spot check, had five updates in a single day. (When compared over a four-month period, four Twitter accounts within the first 25 states surveyed averaged at least three tweets per day.) A very low-frequency account in a very small library might have one update a month; less than that and it's hard to think of the account as other than moribund.

Reach is the extent to which the account is reaching users, and while a library can gain fairly detailed information on its own page's usage, what we can see from outside is the number of likes (for Facebook) or follows (for Twitter). Do you reach half of your potential patrons? This result is improbable for all but the smallest libraries, but a few of those seem to be doing it (six in all, including four already noted and none serving more than 600 patrons). If you are reaching 10 patrons out of 100,000 potential users, that's a sign that you're not doing very well—unless, of course, it's a specialized Facebook account aimed at 10 very powerful benefactors or politicians.

I prepared a five-by-six matrix of codes that combine frequency and reach, based partly on observation and partly on ease of measurement. One axis of that matrix—frequency—tracks the 80/20 rule fairly well. The other—reach—is more ambitious: it represents broader acceptance of library social network accounts than is actually happening. Here are the details.

REACH

It doesn't make sense to use the same measure for reach in a very large library as for a tiny library—or at least it doesn't play out in the real world. What do I mean by that? Here's the second highest percentage of potential patrons as Facebook likes for each HAPLR category (using the second highest because the highest is, in at least one case, implausible except for nonpatron accounts), and using H0 through H9 as convenience codes (used elsewhere in this book):

    H0: Libraries serving fewer than 1,000 people—60.3%
    H1: Libraries serving 1,000 to 2,499 people—40.7%
    H2: Libraries serving 2,500 to 4,999 people—19.9%
    H3: Libraries serving 5,000 to 9,999 people—11.2%
    H4: Libraries serving 10,000 to 24,999 people—9.8%
    H5: Libraries serving 25,000 to 49,999 people—4.6%
    H6: Libraries serving 50,000 to 99,999 people—3.3%
    H7: Libraries serving 100,000 to 249,999 people—3.3%
    H8: Libraries serving 250,000 to 499,999 people—1.3%
    H9: Libraries serving 500,000 or more people—2.3%

There's an obvious trend here—one that's much more obvious when you look at medians or averages. The larger the library, the smaller the percentage of potential patrons it's likely to reach through Facebook or Twitter.

Given that reality, I assigned five reach codes based on numbers that differ based on whether the library is small (H0–H3), medium (H4–H6), or large (H7–H9). They also differ for Facebook and Twitter, being exactly half as high for Twitter since it has fewer than half as many U.S. users. I think of it as the one, two, five, and 10 model, although that may be too simplistic. The codes, their basis, the casual names you might associate with them, and the percentages among 3,141 Facebook pages and 944 Twitter accounts in 38 states are as follows:

a. **Very broad reach.** Facebook: for small libraries, at least 10% of the LSA; for medium libraries, at least 1,000 likes or followers; and for large libraries, at least 3,000 likes or followers. Twitter: 5%, 500, and 1,500, respectively. 4.6% of Facebook pages and 9.7% of Twitter accounts are in category a.

b. **Broad reach.** Facebook: for small libraries, 5 to 9.99% of the LSA; for medium libraries, 500 to 999 likes or followers; and for large libraries, 1,500 to 2,999 likes or followers. Twitter: 2.5 to 4.99%, 250 to 499, and 750 to 1,499, respectively. 11.2% of Facebook pages and 11.9% of Twitter accounts are in category b.

c. **Fairly broad reach.** Facebook: for small libraries, 2.5 to 4.99% of the LSA; for medium libraries, 250 to 499 likes or followers; and for large libraries, 750 to 1,499 likes or followers. Twitter: 1.25 to 2.49%, 125 to 249, and 375 to 749, respectively. 14.2% of Facebook pages and 18.2% of Twitter accounts are in category c.

d. **Modest reach.** Facebook: for small libraries, 1 to 2.49% of the LSA; for medium libraries, 100 to 249 likes or followers, and for large libraries, 300 to 749 likes or followers. Twitter: 0.5 to 1.24%, 50 to 124, and 150 to 374, respectively. 34.3% of Facebook pages and 23.9% of Twitter accounts are in category d.

e. **Limited reach.** Facebook: for small libraries, less than 1% of the LSA; for medium libraries, fewer than 100 likes or followers; and for large libraries, fewer than 300 likes or followers. Twitter: less than 0.5%, fewer than 50, and fewer than 150, respectively. 24.8% of Facebook pages and 36.3% of Twitter accounts are in category e.

While these five categories don't currently represent 80/20 points, they might do so as aspirational levels. Roughly 20% of Facebook and Twitter accounts reach at least level b, and it's reasonable to assume that the percentage in level e could decline to 20% over time.

In the next chapter you will see that these numbers—3,141 Facebook pages and 944 Twitter accounts—differ from the 3,208 Facebook pages and 953 Twitter accounts quoted there. So, let me explain. For 67 Facebook pages and nine Twitter accounts, I was unable to assign a code. This was true for a variety of reasons, primarily because of pages that didn't yet have five updates or tweets, but also because of some Facebook groups, some protected Twitter accounts, and some other anomalies. You'll see similar variations throughout this book. The percentages are of the 98% of Facebook pages for which metrics are available and which have both updates and likes, and of the 99% of Twitter accounts for which metrics are available and which have both five or more tweets and at least one follow.

FREQUENCY AND CURRENCY

These levels are the same for all libraries, although you wouldn't expect most small libraries to reach the highest levels of frequency. The levels are designed to make intuitive sense—but also to make quick measurements easy, as they're based on looking at the five most recent updates or tweets in an account. These levels use numbers, so that the combination of reach and frequency can be a two-character code, from a1 through e6.

1. **Very frequent.** At least five updates per week or 22 per month, most recently updated within the past week. 20.9% of Facebook pages and 32.3% of Twitter accounts fall into this category.
2. **Frequent.** Five updates per fortnight (two weeks) or 11 to 21 per month, most recently updated within the past fortnight. 19.5% of Facebook pages and 18.5% of Twitter accounts fall into this category.
3. **Active.** Five to 10 updates per month, most recently updated within the past month. 22.7% of Facebook pages and 19.6% of Twitter accounts fall into this category.
4. **Infrequent.** Five updates within the last quarter (1.7 per month), most recently updated within the last month. 17.9% of Facebook pages and 12.8% of Twitter accounts fall into this category.
5. **Occasional (primarily here for very small libraries).** Five updates within the last six months (0.8 per month), most recently updated within the last quarter. 8.0% of Facebook pages and 5.5% of Twitter accounts fall into this category.
6. **Moribund or defunct (or too new to categorize).** Either fewer than five updates total, five updates going back more than six months, or the most recent update more than a quarter old. 11.0% of Facebook pages and 11.2% of Twitter accounts fall into this category.

Although assigned theoretically, these categories come close to the 80/20 model at least for Facebook—noting that just under 21% of Facebook pages fall in category 1 and 19% fall into the two troublesome categories, 5 and 6.

You'll find tables showing the numbers and percentages for each reach/frequency combination in chapters 4 (for Facebook) and 5 (for Twitter), along with more comments on some of the high and low spots. As a general comment, I would suggest that any library in the top three categories (in either direction) is doing well with its social networking, almost certainly succeeding as part of overall library community engagement. That is, if a small library has at least 2.5% of its potential patrons (and others in the community) paying attention and is averaging at least one update or tweet per week, it's probably succeeding—and the same is true for medium libraries with at least 250 likes or 125 followers and large libraries with at least 750 likes or 375 followers.

If you're in the fifth category in either direction, you're either building a new page or account or, I suspect, having some problems or ignoring your social networks. I believe most libraries in the sixth category for frequency (except for a handful that simply haven't *had* five updates or tweets yet) have already given up and that these are ghost pages. We'll say a bit more about ghost pages in chapter 6.

The fourth category is the trickiest one. You're doing neither well nor badly. For small libraries, infrequent updates may be the best you can do and may be sensible for your particular situation, and for any library you're getting *some* publicity and possibly engagement. Are you succeeding? That's your call—and given the sheer number of libraries in this area (more than 900 Facebook pages fall into the fourth category in one direction and one of the first four in the other), it's a call many libraries should be considering.

·Self-Identified Successes·

Of the 43 public libraries represented by direct feedback to my query about how libraries felt about their social network accounts, 32 clearly regarded their efforts as successful. (I believe the same claim could be made for all but two or three of the others, but the comments were more ambiguous.)

While 32 libraries barely even rise to the level of anecdata, it's still worth considering the set of libraries and their use of social networks. You'll find comments from librarians at most of the 32 libraries scattered throughout this book. What follows is a statistical profile of the group as a whole.

SIZE AND REACH

The 32 libraries potentially serve a total of just over three million people. They include one library serving fewer than 1,000 people (H0), two serving 2,500 to 4,999 (H2), and four serving 5,000 to 9,999 (H3), for a total of seven small libraries. Six serve 10,000 to 24,999 people (H4), nine serve 25,000 to 49,999 (H5), and three serve 50,000 to 99,999 (H6)—thus 18, more than half of the total, are medium-sized (medium) libraries. Finally, two serve 100,000 to 249,999 (H7), four serve 250,000 to 499,999 (H8), and one serves more than half a million people (H9), for a total of seven large libraries (oddly enough equal to the number of small libraries). Those seven include three non-U.S. public libraries, one each in Canada, New Zealand, and Australia.

Given that people in these libraries all volunteered responses, it's hardly surprising that 100% of the libraries had Facebook pages in late summer 2011 (when first checked) and 18 had Twitter accounts. Those numbers were the same four months later—again not surprisingly.

In the fall 2011 scan, the 32 libraries had a total of 16,424 likes (an average of 0.5% of the LSA, with a median of 0.9%); the 18 with Twitter accounts had a total of 9,982 followers (an average of 0.3% and a median of 0.5%). Median growth for both Facebook likes and Twitter followers was 14% over three months (averages a little higher than that). The median for tweets over the quarter was 5.6 per month, a little more than one per week; the median Twitter account followed 60% as many people as were following it, and those 18 libraries had about 28% as many followers as likes.

But those are averages and medians and as such are misleading even within this small, self-selected group. Let's look at some other details of this group:

- All 18 Twitter accounts were findable directly from the library's home page—but that wasn't true for Facebook pages, where I found six of the pages via Google rather than from the home pages. Notably, five of those six were libraries that apparently did *not* have Twitter accounts.
- Facebook likes ranged from 2,041 down to 41; likes as percentage of LSA range from 11 to 0.1%, with just under half the libraries exceeding 1%. Twitter followers ranged from 1,653 down to 10, with percentages ranging from 4.5% to a percentage that rounded to 0.0% (186 followers from a potential patron base of 446,876, or 0.04%).
- While one library more than doubled its Facebook likes during the quarter, the others ranged from 36% growth down to 1% growth (no library lost likes overall), with actual numbers ranging from 262 (21% growth) down to six (two libraries, representing 9.5% and 2.3% growth, respectively).

- Growth in Twitter followers ranged from a high of 45% (the second highest being 30%) to a low of 3%; actual numbers ranged from 215 (the 45% growth) to a single added follower (11% growth—the smallest Twitter account).
- Actual tweets per month ranged from 328 (a little more than 10 per day) down to 3.5 (a little less than one per week), but a majority of libraries tweeted anywhere from one tweet every other day to two per day.
- Four libraries with Twitter accounts followed more other Twitter accounts than followed them (in one case, more than half again as many). Seven followed less than half as many—and one (but only one out of 18) didn't follow other Twitter accounts at all.
- For six of the 18 tweeting libraries, Twitter appeared to be the more important account with more followers than likes, in one case more than three times as many. Statistically, that contrasts with four cases with fewer than one follower for every three likes—in one case, fewer than one per 10.
- I did one more test on this group of 32 that I didn't do for the whole survey: a quick count of the number of nonlibrary comments within the most recent 10 Facebook posts. (By nonlibrary comments I mean comments that aren't library responses to patron comments or comments clearly from library staff or other libraries.) That number was never more than one per post, but seven of 32 libraries had at least five comments for 10 posts (including one with nine and two with eight). Another four libraries had four comments on 10 posts; two had three; six had two (that is, an average of one comment on every five posts), and six had one. Eight of the 32 libraries—one-quarter of a group that all consider their social networking successful—had no comments in the most recent 10 posts.
- I did mark "interactivity" for all libraries—looking for at least one comment or nonlibrary post within the immediately visible Facebook wall (usually 30 or more posts, which I switched to show everybody's posts where that was an option) and at least one "@" or RT or something of the sort on Twitter pages. Within this group, all but one had *some* comments on Facebook pages; the exception had likes on specific posts but no comments. I found clear evidence of interactivity on only eight of the 18 Twitter streams, but that's not a particularly reliable figure.
- Then there are the reach/frequency codes. For Facebook, 21 of the 32 libraries had reaches in the top three of five categories (with three in the bottom category), and only three libraries fell into the bottom three frequency categories (none in category 6). The two biggest clusters (five libraries each) were b1 (broad reach, very frequent) and d1 (moderate reach, very frequent).
- Among the 18 tweeting libraries, the codes are more concentrated. Thirteen of the 18 fell into the first three reach categories (one in the fifth)—and only one fell below the first three frequency categories, with precisely half in category 1 (very frequent). The biggest cluster with four libraries was c1: fairly broad reach, very frequent.

Librarians at all 32 of these libraries regard their social networking efforts as successful. I believe they're right. It's quite a varied lot for such a small sample, and despite the benchmarks in this book, it reinforces the basic message: Your own measures are what count for your library, and while you could probably do better, if you believe you're succeeding you probably are.

·Doing a Social Network Audit·

Whether your library already has a Facebook or Twitter account or you're thinking of starting one, it probably makes sense to do a web and social network audit every year or so. I'm not suggesting a hugely detailed, expensively documented process that will take hours and yield a formal report. I'm suggesting a quick, informal process that should take less than half an hour but will give you a sense of what's happening now—and another process that may give you a sense of where you should go from here.

DIGRESSION: ONE PROBLEM WITH LIBRARY WEBSITES

This book is not about library websites—and it's not intended to be critical of specific library social networking practices, although indirect criticism may be implicit in much of what I say.

There's a substantial issue with community Facebook pages that appear to be library pages but aren't owned or maintained by the libraries, and it's a problem I can't intelligently comment on. It's also clearly a problem for libraries in some cases, as you'll see *real* Facebook pages under a slightly altered name because the proper name already exists. That's a Facebook management issue and may partly fall into the "you get what you pay for" theory of customer service. How big is the issue? Among the 5,958 libraries checked, more than 1,000 have community Facebook pages that do not appear to have any connection to the libraries themselves. That count includes only libraries that *do not* have findable Facebook pages; I'd guess another 1,000 or more Community Pages exist among the more than 3,000 libraries that have legitimate library Facebook pages. (Libraries may be able to address this issue directly; see chapter 4.)

Here, however, I'm dealing with one specific problem: finding a library's website and making sure it *is* the library's website. Feeling lucky? This is quite possibly a bad idea where public libraries are concerned (especially the smaller libraries that constitute the majority of America's public libraries), because the site you get may very well not be a site run by the library.

There are a *lot* of websites associated with the names of public libraries, and most of those pages appear to exist either for the sake of advertising (as do most autogenerated Facebook Community Pages) or for other unclear purposes. The ones most likely to appear *before* a smaller library's actual website come from Marshall Breeding's Library Technology Guides, and these pages do have useful information and sometimes-outdated links to the real websites. But there are so many others—Yelp pages, Patch pages, Yahoo! pages, publiclibraries.com, Manta's truly mysterious, apparently autogenerated pages, yellowpages, insiderpages, another public libraries directory, epodunk.com, Online Highways pages, local chambers of commerce pages that *claim* to be the official city sites, and more. As part of a much longer discussion in the October 2011 *Cites & Insights*, I offered this partial list and quick commentary:

> Citysearch, epodunk, manta, yelp, yellowpages, awesomebusinesspages, myareaguide, corporationwiki, city-data, ohwy, userinstinct, citytowninfo . . . the list seems endless. Add to that the supposed directories: 50states, publiclibraries.com, publiclibraries.org, educationbug, educationhq . . .

> Problems arise when a user can't locate the official library website among all the crap in search results—and, much as I like lib-web-cats, its tendency to appear *before* actual library websites makes me unhappy. Real problems also arise when it's just not clear what the official website is—or whether there is such a thing.

Did I mention real library and city websites that don't bother to mention the state? Is it obvious to a user where Salem or Johnson County or Lincoln is located? (There's even more than one Livermore in the United States, although the eight Livermores and one Livermore Falls pale in comparison to 34 Salems, 30-odd Lincolns, and a dozen Johnson counties.) All of this may seem irrelevant to this book, except that finding the *right* public library's home page and Facebook or Twitter accounts can be even more cumbersome.

End of digression. Let's get back to the quick, informal web and social network audit. The audit does relate to how I checked the libraries in 38 states, as detailed in the appendix.

FIND YOUR LIBRARY

First, you should find your library's website using standard web search engines—I'd recommend trying both Bing and Google, and I'd also recommend trying both a phrase search for the name you actually use and a word search (in both cases, adding a state helps cut down on clutter and is *essential* if your library is in Salem or Lincoln).

Ideally, your official website should be the first result in all four cases (that is, word and phrase searches on Google and Bing). This assumes that your library has a website, and it appears that hundreds (possibly thousands) of mostly smaller libraries do not. That's always unfortunate. Credit goes to Plinkit and other statewide initiatives for bringing many smaller libraries web pages that though not terribly fancy are workable and apparently maintainable. Other libraries have used blogs as their websites (with Wordpress, a "blog" can actually be a very sophisticated website), and it's plausible to use a Facebook page as a library website.

If your library's website comes in on top in all four cases, great. If not, what appears before it and can you determine *why* you're not number one? Your library may well have books on search engine optimization (SEO); if not, SEO advice is easy to come by, if not always useful. It helps if your library's website clearly identifies the library not only at the top of the visible home page but also in the page's title (in the page's metadata).

For that matter, does your library have one *and only one* clearly identified home page? I've seen a few dozen cases where two different sites both appeared to be the primary library website. (Sometimes one site is a page from the parent political body; sometimes it's a canned site that may have come with your online catalog and long since been forgotten. There may be other situations as well.) If your library can change other sites so they link to the primary website (effectively acting as aliases), that's probably the ideal solution.

Again, it's not my intention to critique library websites and home pages here. I will add one question, however: Does the home page (and preferably every other page on your website) clearly identify the *city and state* (or for some regional libraries, at least the state) you're located in? I wouldn't ask the question if there weren't cases where the state didn't appear on the home page. Even if you're certain that there's no other Pierce County Library System, it doesn't hurt to add a clear state identification. (That's *not* one of the known examples: The system headquartered in Tacoma, Washington, has its state clearly identified at the bottom of the home page—and the one in Elmwood, Wisconsin, is equally clear.)

FIND YOUR FACEBOOK PAGE(S)

Does your library's home page have a clear, unambiguous link to your Facebook page? I don't mean that cute little "Like" symbol that signs up a patron to like the page without seeing it; I mean something that will get them there.

Most commonly, that means an icon—either the Facebook "f" (which I've seen in sizes all the way down to a single text character) or one of the "Like us on Facebook" or "Find us on Facebook" or similar messages. If you're dead set against commercial icons on your home page (a sentiment I can support), a text link will also do.

There is a reason I ask this question. When I went looking for Facebook pages, I found more than 1,880 linked directly from library home pages, but I found *another* 1,300 via Google—pages that had no apparent links that I could find. (There were also 20 that didn't show up in the first 100 Google results but that could be found searching directly in Facebook.)

Chapter 6 includes some discussion of this issue, including a successful (and high profile) library making the case that a link from the home page isn't needed. For most libraries, however, it seems like a good idea.

Whether or not you have a visible, *working* link (there are some icons on library home pages that don't work properly), you should also check the first 100 or so Google results for other Facebook pages. You may be surprised by what you find. There are many, many Community Pages libraries had nothing to do with. You may be able to claim those for your library and link them to your real Facebook page—or, if you don't yet have one, you may be able to claim one and turn it into the library Facebook page (see chapter 4). You may also find autogenerated pages because your library has a Wikipedia article or for other reasons.

You might also find a true library Facebook page that the library has forgotten about—possibly one created by a short-term employee who left the library or one created as a volunteer's project and lost in the shuffle. If you're able to find the access information, consider whether you should restart the page or at least provide a suitable final message. See chapter 6 for more on this.

FIND YOUR TWITTER ACCOUNT

What goes for Facebook also goes for Twitter, except that you're a lot less likely to have a Twitter account already—and there are no autogenerated Twitter accounts. When I checked, most Twitter accounts did have links on library home pages—nearly 800 out of a total 953. The rest either showed up via Google or could be found only by searching directly in Twitter.

Here again, don't assume that you do *not* have a Twitter account. Twitter's been around longer than you may assume, almost as long as Facebook's been open to the public. There are quite a few Twitter accounts that appear to have been abandoned; some of those accounts haven't had a tweet in more than two years. Do you have any way of recovering the account information, so you can either close the account, restart it, or at least provide a proper "we're not tweeting anymore" tweet?

If you're involved in other social networks, the same steps apply. Do you have a MySpace account that you'd forgotten about? Should you even try to recover it? Are you starting a Google+ page, or are you one of the few libraries that has already done so?

CONSIDER YOUR PEERS

The steps above probably took you less time to do than to read about. The next step may involve reading the rest of this book and supplemental reports (if issued). You should probably see how peer libraries are doing on Twitter and Facebook, either as part of considering whether to open or update accounts or as part of making your social networking even more effective.

What's a peer? I'd suggest at least two axes of similarity: libraries in your size category (either broad categories such as small, medium, and large or more granular categories such as the HAPLR numbers) and libraries in your state or region. Chapters 3 (for size) and 7 (for state) provide some overall benchmarks and library names that may help get you started.

SEE HOW YOU'RE DOING

Look at your numbers—the ones directly available on the page and those that you can find as the account owner. Look at the pages and accounts themselves. If you've established a baseline, compare where you are now to where you were a year or six months ago. You might choose to classify your library using the reach/frequency code in this book, or you might not.

Are you happy with the results? If your library is anywhere in the a1–c3 range (that is, a1, a2, a3, b1, b2, b3, c1, c2, c3), there's a pretty good chance you *are* happy with how things are going, but that's up to you to decide.

Looking at your Facebook page, are you getting an appropriate level of feedback? If you're directly asking questions or polls and getting no comments or responses, that's unfortunate; it may speak either to your community or to the tone of your page.

If there are comments and specifically questions, is the library responding rapidly and in human voices? If you find specific questions that go unanswered, is it because nobody's monitoring the page or because your rules for Facebook and Twitter are too restrictive?

Are you finding spam on your pages? If a comment on a story hour is an author's description of a self-published (or AuthorHouse related) book that's not relevant to the specific story hour, *that's spam*. If an author outside your community posts a stand-alone comment pushing his or her own book, *that's spam*—at least by my standards. Much worse and not all that unusual, if there are messages saying how people are making big money at home, you can almost always assume those messages are spam (they're most likely to show up on moribund Facebook pages). If you allow spam to remain, you're providing free advertising and damaging your library's standing.

Are you continuing to attract new followers and likes, or has your account flatlined? If you're seeing very little growth or even starting to lose patrons, can you determine why? Is it possible that you're updating too often or including too much content that followers don't care about? Is it possible that your library's voice is too institutional?

CONSIDER WHAT MAKES SENSE FOR YOUR LIBRARY

Every library is different. That should be obvious but sometimes needs to be said. Each library has its own community (with different levels of social networking involvement and awareness), its own resources, and its own priorities.

For some libraries, social networking just isn't worth the effort, and that can be true for libraries that already have Facebook pages or Twitter accounts. Maybe the hours spent updating those accounts really would be better spent preparing e-mail newsletters, responding to questions on your physical bulletin board, or going out into the community with other forms of outreach. Or maybe those hours just don't exist.

Don't try to ramp up too rapidly or too heavily. Does it really make sense for your medium-sized library to have six updates a day on a Facebook page? For that matter, does it make sense for any library to have that many updates? Do you really want to force all updates through a single chain of command, or would you benefit from multiple, possibly signed or initialed contributors?

Do you need one, both, or more social presences? I wonder a little about the Twitter feeds that are nothing more than truncated versions of Facebook updates. But I wonder even more about Facebook pages that appear to be pure mirrors of Twitter accounts.

Don't assume that what's right for your peers is right for you. Don't try to emulate a high-profile large library when you're running a small library with a tiny staff augmented by volunteers or when you're running an entirely volunteer library. Do what works for you.

ACT ON YOUR DECISION OF WHAT YOU NEED

I don't think it makes sense to build a detailed strategic plan for social networking, although some large libraries may find it necessary. I think it makes sense to make sure you have enough buy-in to keep things going for a while, do a quick social network audit, and act.

Open the Facebook or Twitter account (you don't need Facebook first—some libraries use *only* Twitter with considerable success) or restart the moribund account if that makes sense. Fill in the information as needed, being as clear and expansive as possible.

Then start tweeting or updating. Monitor the account to see what happens. Engage your community when it engages the library. Don't expect miracles, but do plan for involvement and growth.

And at least once a year do a new audit. See how things are going, whether you need to make adjustments, whether some new network is beginning to look like a winner in your community, or whether an existing account no longer serves your needs.

Social networking isn't free, although the costs are primarily labor rather than direct expenses. It can be enormously rewarding in making your library more human, integrating it even more closely into your community, and engaging many of your patrons in a way that should make them stronger supporters of your library. That won't always happen, and sometimes social networking fails, but the odds are on your side.

CHAPTER 3

· · · · · · · · ·

THE BIG PICTURE AND THE SMALLER PICTURE

JUST AS NO single model makes sense for all libraries considering or using social networks, no single number or set of numbers adequately describes the status quo. This chapter and chapters 7 and 8 look at some of the numbers, both for the overall situation and for subsets of the library population. Subsets considered in this chapter are size categories. Chapter 7 looks at each state among the 38 surveyed. Chapter 8 considers changes in library social networking in 25 states over a four-month period.

· The Majority Issue: True Both Ways ·

Most public libraries within the 38 states surveyed (and probably most public libraries in the United States as a whole) were present on Facebook. Most public libraries were *not* active on Facebook. While 53.9% of the 5,958 libraries in 38 states had either a page, a profile, or a group on Facebook, 344 of those pages hadn't had an update in more than three months—they were wholly inactive by most standards. Subtracting the 344 pages gives you 48.1% of the libraries with active Facebook pages.

Twitter-only libraries didn't make up the difference; there were only 57 of them, and 16 of those were inactive Twitter accounts with no tweet in at least three months. That leaves a total of 2,907 libraries that appeared to be actively involved in social networking, or 48.8% of the total.

If you're wondering how much these numbers might change if the other 12 states were included, the only answer is that there's no way of knowing. If I project the percentage of social network users for each size category of public library to the libraries not yet surveyed—which is *not* an entirely reasonable thing to do—I'd come up with just over 51% of all 9,184 public libraries having Facebook accounts. Even if none of the other accounts were inactive—which seems highly unlikely—the total of active Facebook pages, groups, and accounts still wouldn't be half of all libraries. If you adopt a slightly tighter definition of "active"—say that a page needs to be updated at least once a month and needs to have some minimum number of likes or followers—the activity percentage drops significantly. I calculate 2,073 Facebook pages, or just under 35% of the public libraries in the 38 states.

In other words, it's factual to say either that roughly one-third of libraries in the survey were active on social networks, that just under half were, or that just over half were. But it's also factual to say that, *when defined by service area,* nearly four out of five potential library users are served by libraries on social networks—78.7% to be precise. I say "factual" rather than true because the truth is a little fuzzy . . . especially given one other factor: the total of all likes in all library Facebook pages in 38 states is just under one million people, and the total of Twitter followers is just under 300,000. That means that across the board only half of 1% of library patrons like their library's Facebook pages, and one-quarter of 1% of library patrons (for libraries with Twitter accounts) follow their library's Twitter accounts.

You could look at those numbers and conclude that public libraries are massively failing at social networking—after all, more than 99% of potential patrons didn't sign up. That's also factual but, I believe, not meaningful. Maybe what follows will help.

· The Nature of the Sample ·

This book is based on an external study of all the public libraries in 38 states, just under two-thirds of all U.S. public libraries and including libraries serving more than 246 million people. The states *not* surveyed this time around were Arkansas, Delaware, Hawaii, Illinois, Iowa, Kansas, Michigan, New York, North Dakota, South Dakota, Tennessee, and West Virginia; the District of Columbia is also left out. (The reason for leaving out the first 12 is because at the time I couldn't find downloadable tables of library names and LSA populations from the state libraries.)

Table 3.1 shows the nature of the sample by size of libraries, referring to the latest HAPLR report for total number of libraries in each size category.

The bias is unintentional but also unavoidable. The original 25-state sample, which represented more than half the nation by population, had a much more extreme bias, running from 42% for libraries serving 1,000 to 2,499 people to 162% for libraries serving more than half a million people.

Those of you who are numerically inclined may be noting a fairly smooth series here. L of H, the percentage of all libraries included in this 38-state sample, increases reasonably smoothly as library size increases (although there's a huge jump between the 50,000–99,999 category and the 100,000–249,999 category). Similarly, the bias changes in a regular and predictable manner, with the same huge jump. I don't think there's anything terribly meaningful in either of those. The remaining 12 states aren't all small or lightly populated, but they have many reporting library agencies relative to the sizes of the states. (New York has nearly four times as many reporting libraries as California, even though California has nearly twice as many people, but New York also has some of the nation's largest libraries.)

TABLE 3.1

Libraries in the 38 states, by size

SIZE	H#	H%	LSN	LSN%	L OF H	OV/UND
0: <1,000	1,072	11.7%	531	8.9%	49.53%	−23.6%
1: 1–2.4K	1,524	16.6%	840	14.1%	55.12%	−15.0%
2: 2.5K–4.9K	1,310	14.3%	790	13.3%	60.31%	−7.0%
3: 5K–9.9K	1,483	16.1%	978	16.4%	65.95%	1.7%
4: 10–24K	1,764	19.2%	1,235	20.7%	70.01%	7.9%
5: 25–49K	952	10.4%	688	11.5%	72.27%	11.4%
6: 50–99K	556	6.1%	416	7.0%	74.82%	15.3%
7: 100–249K	335	3.6%	306	5.1%	91.34%	40.8%
8: 250–499K	104	1.1%	96	1.6%	92.31%	42.3%
9: 500K+	84	0.9%	78	1.3%	92.86%	43.1%
TOTAL	9,184		5,958		64.87%	
Rural	7,153	77.9%	4,374	73.4%	61.15%	−5.7%
Urban	2,031	22.1%	1,584	26.6%	77.99%	20.2%
Small	5,389	58.7%	3,139	52.7%	58.25%	−10.2%
Medium	3,272	35.6%	2,339	39.3%	71.49%	10.2%
Large	523	5.7%	480	8.1%	91.78%	41.5%

Note: **Size** is the LSA (legal service area) population, where "K" stands for thousand and "9" is followed by as many other 9s as necessary. Rural, Urban, Small, Medium, and Large are groupings defined in chapter 1 and used throughout this book. **H#** is the number of libraries in that size grouping, according to the latest Hennen's American Public Library Ratings. **H%** is the percentage of *all* libraries in this size category—thus, 16.6% of America's public libraries serve 1,000 to 2,499 people. **LSN** is the number of libraries in this Library Social Network study. **LSN%** is like H%: a vertical percentage, the portion of all libraries in this study that are in this size category. Thus, 1.3% of the libraries in the 38 states potentially serve half a million people or more. **L of H** is simply LSN over H#: the percentage of libraries within the 50 states and DC that are in the 38 states studied. **Ov/Und** is a measure of sample bias: the percent by which this size library is underrepresented (negative figures) or overrepresented.

· Library Social Networking Presence by Libraries ·

Table 3.2 shows the overall presence of Facebook and Twitter accounts by size of library—noting that "presence" here is used in the broadest sense, including hundreds of apparently abandoned accounts as well as some that have no likes or followers and others that have no posts (but appear to be under library control).

If you're having trouble spotting the interesting items in table 3.2, here are some of the things I find noteworthy. For both Twitter and Facebook, the percentage of libraries with a presence on the service increases fairly smoothly as the size of library increases. (In the first 25 states, there was one downward jog in the Facebook series, but that's no longer true—and in the first pass through those 25, none of the smallest libraries had Twitter accounts.) Figure 3.1 shows this increase graphically.

The extremes are interesting in different ways. More than one-fifth of the smallest libraries are on Facebook, and more than one-tenth of the very largest ones do not appear to be, at least for the library or system as a whole. The fact that more than half of the large libraries have Twitter accounts may or may not be surprising.

Consider the clusters. Four out of 10 small libraries have some Facebook presence, as do two-thirds of medium libraries and three-quarters of large libraries. Only one out of 20 small libraries are on Twitter (but there are still 157 such libraries—there are a *lot* of small libraries!), compared to something less than a quarter of medium libraries and more than half of large ones.

FIGURE 3.1

Twitter and Facebook presence, by size of library

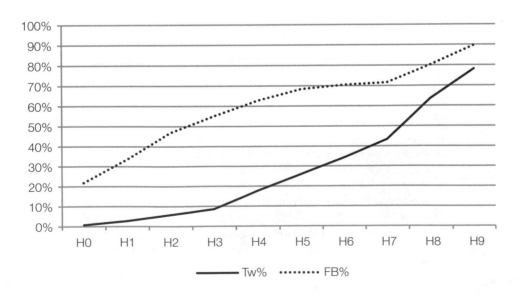

TABLE 3.2

Twitter and Facebook presence, by size of library

SIZE	LSN	TW	FB	BOTH	TW%	FB%	BOTH%
H0	531	4	115	4	0.8%	21.7%	0.8%
H1	840	23	283	20	2.7%	33.7%	2.4%
H2	790	46	370	42	5.8%	46.8%	5.3%
H3	978	84	539	78	8.6%	55.1%	8.0%
H4	1,235	219	774	202	17.7%	62.7%	16.4%
H5	688	179	469	168	26.0%	68.2%	24.4%
H6	416	143	293	138	34.4%	70.4%	33.2%
H7	306	133	218	126	43.5%	71.2%	41.2%
H8	96	61	77	56	63.5%	80.2%	58.3%
H9	78	61	70	60	78.2%	89.7%	76.9%
TOTAL	5,958	953	3,208	894	16.0%	53.8%	15.0%
Rural	4,374	376	2,081	346	8.6%	47.6%	7.9%
Urban	1,584	577	1,127	548	36.4%	71.1%	34.6%
Small	3,139	157	1,307	144	5.0%	41.6%	4.6%
Medium	2,339	541	1,536	508	23.1%	65.7%	21.7%
Large	480	255	365	242	53.1%	76.0%	50.4%

Note: **Size:** I've used H0–H9 here to conserve space; **LSN:** number of libraries in the 38 states surveyed; **Tw:** libraries for which I located a Twitter account; **FB:** libraries for which I located a Facebook page, excluding friends pages, community pages, and pages for subsets of the patrons (e.g., kids, teens) or individual branches when there's no overall page; **Both:** libraries with both Facebook and Twitter accounts as defined above; **Tw%:** percentage of libraries with Twitter accounts; **FB%:** percentage of libraries with Facebook accounts; **Both%:** percentage of libraries with both.

PRESENCE BY POPULATION

Consider actual population—LSA, the number of potential patrons. Note here and elsewhere in this book that there's some double counting, with people in the legal service area for both a reporting library and a reporting collaborative of libraries.

Table 3.3 shows how many potential patrons are served by libraries with Facebook and Twitter accounts, respectively. *Population* is the total population (LSA) served by libraries in a size category within the 38 states; *Facebook* and *Twitter* are the total population served by libraries with some presence in that network, even if it's an abandoned account. *FB%* and *Tw%* are those figures divided by overall population. In other words, half of the people in these 38 states *could* follow their libraries on Twitter (if the people use Twitter), but that's true for less than 1% of those served by the smallest libraries and more than three-quarters of those served by the largest libraries. Similarly, three-quarters of the people *could* like their library's Facebook page (if those people are on Facebook), and that fraction is never lower

TABLE 3.3

Percentage of population served, by libraries
with social network presence

SIZE	POPULATION	FACEBOOK	FB%	TWITTER	TW%
H0	297,922	76,640	25.7%	2,602	0.9%
H1	1,411,186	492,917	34.9%	43,368	3.1%
H2	2,901,996	1,368,816	47.2%	168,833	5.8%
H3	7,127,517	3,940,255	55.3%	626,663	8.8%
H4	19,881,234	12,698,161	63.9%	3,671,763	18.5%
H5	24,256,708	16,517,371	68.1%	6,356,732	26.2%
H6	29,345,301	20,942,256	71.4%	10,503,411	35.8%
H7	48,572,287	34,929,788	71.9%	21,841,887	45.0%
H8	33,384,992	27,148,437	81.3%	21,804,207	65.3%
H9	79,514,058	71,055,399	89.4%	59,900,252	75.3%
TOTAL	**246,693,201**	**189,170,040**	**76.7%**	**124,919,718**	**50.6%**
Rural	31,619,855	18,576,789	58.8%	4,513,229	14.3%
Urban	215,073,346	170,593,251	79.3%	120,406,489	56.0%
Small	11,738,621	5,878,628	50.1%	841,466	7.2%
Medium	73,483,243	50,157,788	68.3%	20,531,906	27.9%
Large	161,471,337	133,133,624	82.5%	103,546,346	64.1%

than one-quarter but goes up to nearly nine out of 10. The percentages consistently rise with larger libraries.

These are *potential* figures. The actual figures are not quite so good. And we'll look at those numbers in chapters 4 and 5.

· Sampling the Sizes ·

Let's look at one or two libraries in each of the 10 size categories—libraries that stand out for popularity, activity, or both. Most of these libraries are from the first states, with updates and tweets retrieved in late summer 2011.

LIBRARIES SERVING FEWER THAN 1,000 PEOPLE

I've already noted Hope and Seldovia in Alaska, Stanley District in Idaho, and Village of Corona in New Mexico, four very small libraries reaching roughly half of their communities via Facebook.

Reserve Public Library in New Mexico, serving 389 people, has 54 likes (14% of the community) and averages roughly a post each month, with periods of much stronger activity. At the time I originally checked it, the community was threatened by a forest fire (the Wallow fire in Arizona), and the updates kept the community informed about this area emergency. Checking the Facebook account in January 2012, it's clear that this is a *very* engaged community resource, with more discussion on the general wall than in the stream of updates from the library itself. Examples from late 2011, with one slightly anonymized:

> Author Audrie Clifford's visit and book signing was a great success. We had nearly a full house. Audrie sent us a lovely thank you note expressing her appreciation for the opportunity to share her new book with us, and to reconnect with old friends in the community. The Library also held a fund-raising bake sale and it was also a great success! A very sincere thank you to everyone that donated the most delicious baked goodies. The Library will be putting several new books on the shelf from the proceeds of the sale.

> On December 10, 2011, at 2 PM the Reserve Public Library is happy to announce we will host visiting author Audrie Clifford, former Mayor of Reserve. She will be sharing excerpts and signing copies of her book "Another Damn Newcomer—Confrontational Politics, Environmental Issues and Fun in Rural New Mexico." Please plan on joining us to welcome Ms Clifford!

> **[Community member]** Would I be able to request 'The Fool's Progress' by Ed Abbey via inter-library loan? October 21, 2011 at 11:46am

> **Reserve Public Library** Thanks for the request. We will get
> that order out today. ILL's usually take week to two to come in.
> October 21, 2011 at 2:43pm
>
> **[Community member]** Thank you so much!! October 21, 2011
> at 9:20pm

Langdon Public Library in New Hampshire serves 751 people. It has both a Facebook page liked by 104 people (13%) and a Twitter account followed by 90 (11%), and the library scores "a1" for both accounts, averaging a post or tweet a day. Here are examples—with feedback—from the last two days of 2011:

> Announcing our top 3 circulating books in 2011! #3 James Patterson's
> "Toys" #2 "A Dog's Purpose" by W. Bruce Cameron and . . . #1 "The
> Help" by Kathryn Stockett! **3 people like this.**
>
> > **Dave** Always interesting to know. Happy New Year, and may there
> > be much more good reading and good books in 2012!

> Announcing the top 3 circulating DVDs at the Langdon Library in 2011!
> #3 Dinner for Schmucks #2 The Social Network and . . . #1 The King's
> Speech! **2 people like this.**

> We're officially calling it. At year's end we have served a total of 8014
> (hopefully) happy patrons! Just 6 shy of last year's record. We're going
> to go ahead and call that a win. Happy New Year, Everyone!! **8 people
> like this.**

Most tweets appear to be Facebook updates autotruncated to fit Twitter.

LIBRARIES SERVING 1,000 TO 2,499 PEOPLE

The David M. Hunt Library in Falls Village, Connecticut (1,095), has 216 friends for its Facebook account (20% of the community)—a personal account rather than an organizational page—and appears to average about three updates a week. There's strong engagement. Following are a few (edited) items from this unusual account:

> David M. Hunt created an event. The Natural World—: a 12"X12" Group
> Exhibition of Local Artist Reception Saturday, September 17, 2011 at
> 5:00pm

> "Hope you are coming to this . . ." on Robin Cockerline's post on The Natural
> World—: a 12"X12" Group Exhibition of Local Artist Reception's wall.

"Thank you for that Lori you are . . ." on The Natural World—: a
12"X12" Group Exhibition of Local Artist Reception's Wall.

David M. Hunt created an event. Audubon Reptile Day! Tuesday at
2:00pm David M. Hunt Library, Falls Village, Connecticut

"Ooohhh . . . can't wait to see them . . ." on John Dildine's post on CALL
FOR ARTISTS' WORK—THE NATURAL WORLD's wall.

The Williamsport–Washington Township Public Library in Indiana serves 2,351 people and, when checked in late October 2011, had 379 likes for its Facebook page (16%), a page averaging roughly an update every other day. It's also strong on community involvement, as hinted at by these three updates in mid-December 2011:

Thank you to everyone who volunteered tonight and donated goodies
to the library! If you had your picture taken with Santa, don't forget
to stop by the library next week and get a copy of your photo! **Kathy
likes this.**

Julia The Open House was wonderful! Thank you.

Santa's comin' tonight, tonight! Library Open House party starts at 4!
Suzie likes this.

Suzie I can't wait till then!!

The Friends are raffling off a quilt and recliner at the Open House! 1
ticket for $1 or 7 tickets for $5. Drawing will be held on January 6th.
Thank you to Rusty M. for your donation!

LIBRARIES SERVING 2,500 TO 4,999 PEOPLE

Winnebago Public Library in Minnesota serves 2,814 people and had both a Facebook account with 139 likes (4.5% of the community) and a Twitter account with 27 followers in December 2011—and both accounts had frequent activity, seeming to average more than two updates per day. In a cursory scan, the tweets appeared to be the same as the updates (but shorter). Following are three excerpted updates, including a sample of the community engagement:

Full house at the Family Event: Summer Reading Program Pajama Party!
tonight! Thanks for coming! Hope you enjoyed Gnomeo & Juliet! . . .

Monday! Today's the last day of the Summer Reading Program. Join us for our Family Event: Summer Reading Program Pajama Party! We'll be watching Gnomeo & Juliet! **3 people like this.**

> **Mackenzie** ha i passed out watching that movie

> **Muir Library** Well, come help me serve popcorn tonight and then we can watch it on the bigscreen together

> **Sherry** Can't wait! We'll be there!

We're open for another hour this morning! Stop in for a weekend magazine, movie or book!

Manitou Springs Public Library in Colorado had 605 likes for its active Facebook page in December 2011 (12% of the LSA) and a little more than one update per day. The wall was an interesting mix of events and initial portions of distinctly personal book reviews, as in this set of four updates (all from the same day, slightly excerpted):

FINAL LAWN CONCERT! We wanted to go out with a bang, so what better way to do that than invite Molly Boyles and Lipstick Voodoo? Don't miss this special event, rain or shine! . . . **Miramont Castle likes this.**

Cool Science Guy Marc Straub will make ice cream with the kids at Tuesday night's final lawn concert. Meet with him at 5:30, grab some ice cream, and listen to the music! **[Wall Photos]**

Saint Iggy by K. L. Going Well this WAS NOT a paranormal book like I thought it would be. That's what I get for just looking at the cover. It was however a good book. After an incident Iggy gets kicked out of high school and there is no one to tell, his mother has gone off AGAIN, his dad is passed out on the couch, the phone is disconnected. . . . **[Link]**

Lies that Chelsea Handler Told Me by Chelsea's Family and Friends OH SO FUNNY! I lost count of the times I laughed out loud! It's hard to believe people stay friends with her, because she can be so awful but it's really funny to read about. I guess she's very generous and takes everyone on vacation with her so maybe the humiliation is worth it. Apparently she can lie to you with a straight face and get everyone around you to lie too. This book is just tales told by the people closest to her, of her lies and pranks on them. . . . **[Link]**

LIBRARIES SERVING 5,000 TO 9,999 PEOPLE

Bisbee, Arizona's Copper Queen Library serves 6,423 people, 650 of them (10%) liking the very active Facebook page (averaging two updates per day) with a wide range of updates, not all of them directly related to the library. Examples from early August 2011 include:

> An excellent article from Macleans Magazine on Vancouver, BC's MacLeod's, "surely Canada's finest antiquarian bookstore. . . ." The last great bookshop [Link]

> > **Emilie** I fear I would get lost for days . . . weeks

> Just in time for the various weekend book sections . . . Funny! Book Reviews Demystified [Link]

> Scary stuff! ;-) Copper Queen Library: What's New?: Booklist's "Top 10 Horror Fiction: 2011" [Link]

> "Never confuse movement with action."—Ernest Hemingway . . . **Scott Christian likes this.**

Cameron Parish Library in Louisiana serves 6,584 people and had 1,100 friends (17%) on its traditional Facebook account in early December 2011. There aren't huge numbers of updates, but the library's strong on noting interesting books—and getting reactions. For example:

> A VERY Popular Book at the Cameron Library! Heaven is for Real: A Little Boy's Astounding Story of His Trip to Heaven and Back, Deluxe Edition. . . . **4 people like this.**

> > **Donna** Excellent reading!!

> > **Drama** this is a very good book . . . i can also recommend "The Traveler's Gift" by Andy Andrews . . . not sure if cameron has It, but cal par library does. . . .

> > **Stella Ann** That is an awesome book!!

> > **Darlene** Awesome book.

LIBRARIES SERVING 10,000 TO 24,999 PEOPLE

In my own three-way split, this bracket marks the beginning of medium-sized libraries, but it's also the end of the "rural" category. The Casey County Public Library in Liberty, Kentucky, serves 16,498 people and has 1,611 likes (9.8%) for its Facebook page, which is updated a couple of times a week. Here are excerpted updates from August 2011, including direct questions to engage the community:

> Question for you—what was your favorite book when you were a child?
> **Yesterday at 4:43pm. 3 people like this.**
>
> > **Elizabeth Diane** One of my favorite books as a child was "Monster at the end of this book" and I was a fan of the little engine that could. . . . I remember in middle school my favorite book was Joan Lowery Nixon's *The Name of the Game was Murder.*
> >
> > **Elizabeth Diane** I have also read my favorite little critter books and two specific books, "The Velveteen Rabbit" & "I Love You Stinkyface" to my nephew growing up. I like to pass books down. I've even written originals for my nephews. **About an hour ago**

> 7 pm MOVIE this Saturday—SEASON OF THE WITCH! (rated PG-13) Remember, FREE admission, FREE popcorn on a big 12 foot x 12 foot cinema screen & surround sound stereo system in air conditioned comfort! **[Link] Charles likes this.**
>
> > **Christine** I really wanted to view this movie tonight but other things have come up. Is this movie available in the library to reserve?
> >
> > **Casey County Public Library** it will be after it is played, Christine—give us a little while to get it processed & we'll put it on hold for you & call you when it's ready!

> We would like to say THANKS THANKS THANKS to our two tireless Saturday volunteers: ANNE STREETER & BILLYE WATSON! Most every week these 2 lovely ladies can be found popping corn & pouring soda for the 1 pm movie at your library! What do we say to them on those days (like today) when we get 50+ people? THANKS THANKS THANKS! **10 people like this.**

The Wareham Free Library serves 21,349 people in Massachusetts and had 2,026 likes (9.5%) for its Facebook page in October 2011. The Facebook page isn't updated all that often but does keep the community informed; it's a good example of an infrequently updated page with strong reach. Examples covering two months include:

> Spooky Story Night—Thursday at 6:30pm. Be here if you're not too scared!!!! **October 25, 2011. 2 people like this.**

Today is the day—Friends Day at Chili's (Cranberry Highway) until 11pm tonight. Be sure to bring your flier and Chili's will donate 10% of their sales to the Friends. Hope to see you there. Fliers are available at the library or @ warehamfreelibrary.org **October 5, 2011. Jeanne likes this.**

e Reader Q & A at WFL presented by James Hanrahan from Best Buy. 10/7 at 11am or 10/12 at 6pm. Come and try out an e Reader or bring your own for hands on instruction. Register at the library. **September 28, 2011. 2:51pm**

Last chance for Open Mike Night—Wednesday August 31—5:30–7:30 in the library courtyard. We have had some awesome local talent these past weeks—come and join in the fun. **August 29, 2011**

LIBRARIES SERVING 25,000 TO 49,999 PEOPLE

The Libraries of Stevens County (Washington), also known as the Stevens County Rural Library District, may fit into the smallest "urban" size category with 43,830 population—but that's across more than half a dozen locations. The overall Facebook account had 1,538 likes (3.5%) and roughly one update per day in early December 2011. Examples from earlier that year include:

What a literate place Stevens County is! Just saw a guy wearing a t-shirt in the Hunters Library that said: "I'm so adjective, I verb nouns." **4 people like this.**

> **Debbie** I just saw a t-shirt that said "Trust me!" look at this picture and tell me what this might be.

> **Debbie** Remember, I'm at a psychology conference and Rorschach tests are ink blots. A psych sense of humor.

If you, or someone you know, has questions or comments about the library levy, contact the Library Director directly via this online form, by email, or give her a call! Levy Comments and Suggestions librariesofstevenscounty.org We welcome all of your comments and questions. **[Contact Info and Form] 3 people like this.**

> **Linda** What a treasure this library system is, please vote for this levy!!

Tuesday at the Kettle Falls Public Library at 10:30 "Library Youth Garden" (ages 6-Teen). Join us for a little weeding and then painting rocks for garden decorations.

Bozeman Public Library (Montana), serving 47,805 people, had both a (relatively recent) Twitter account with 78 followers and a Facebook account with around three updates a week and 1,414 likes (3%) as of December 2011. The two streams sometimes differ and sometimes cover the same topics. For example, here are three tweets from August 2011:

1447 people visited your library yesterday! Don't forget to bring in your reading logs and book reviews for prizes through August 15!

The 4th annual One Book—One Bozeman is just around the corner! Listen to the author Aron Ralston read Between a . . . **[Link]**

Stop in for a cool drink and a refreshing read on your way to the Sweet Pea and SLAM Festivals! 6 Aug

overlap with these three updates from the same days:

The 4th annual One Book—One Bozeman is just around the corner! Listen to the author Aron Ralston read *Between a Rock and Hard Place* on CD. Watch 127 Hours starring James Franco. Check out 15 copies in a book kit for your discussion group. Get ready to join in the discussion and events taking place in September! **[Link] Monday at 5:04am. 3 people like this.**

As part of the Montana State Library's BTOP (Broadband Technologies Opportunities Program) grant, the Library has recently added ZoomText software. This enables users to magnify the computer screen to a variety of sizes, and is useful for many people with visual difficulties. ZoomText has been installed on the Library's two ADA accessible computers. Please call 582–2941 if you have any questions. msl.mt.gov msl.mt.gov **Debra Bungo likes this.**

Would you like to receive the Library's monthly newsletter online? Follow the link below to sign up! You can also sign up for new book lists and Library Board agenda and minutes. **[Link] Abundant Health Family Chiropractic Bozeman likes this.**

LIBRARIES SERVING 50,000 TO 99,999 PEOPLE

Allegany County Library System serves 72,831 people in Maryland and has both Twitter and Facebook accounts, generally with the same information at fairly frequent intervals; the accounts have 123 followers and 301 likes, respectively (0.4%). These are sample updates (all from one day) from a stream that seems primarily event-driven:

> Family Law Self Help Center today from 4:30 to 6:30 at the Frostburg Library.

> Computer Class: Photo Editing with Picasa—What do you do with all those digital photos? We will explore Picasa, a free software download from Google that makes it easy and fun to view, organize, edit and share the digital photos on your PC. Frostburg Branch today at 11AM **Sharron likes this.**

> *Never let me go* [videorecording] (R)—Review by: Chris Title: Never let me go Starring: Andrew Garfield, Cha. **[Link]**

California's Santa Monica Public Library serves 92,703 people and also has both Twitter (1,142 followers, 1.2%) and Facebook (2,041 likes, 2.2%) accounts with similar but not identical content. Here are four tweets from July 2011:

> E.T. actress & author Dee Wallace visits the Main Library to discuss her book 'Bright Light' and her spiritual journey. **Tues, 7/26, 7 pm**

> For NetLibrary users: The way to get Recorded Books online has changed. Go to **[Link]** to create your new free User ID.

> What's this year's Teen Summer Reading Club GRAND PRIZE? Check out the Teen Blog for the answer and other details. **[Link]**

> To help you through Carmageddon SMPL will be open normal operating hours this weekend (7/16–7/17) **[Link]**

"Carmageddon" in this case is not the violent videogame that Wikipedia discusses, but a supposed weekend traffic nightmare that occurred when 10 miles of I-405 (or, if you're a Southern Californian, the 405) were shut down for a July weekend. For whatever reasons, most people stayed away and the nightmare never happened.

LIBRARIES SERVING 100,000 TO 249,999 PEOPLE

Now we're getting to libraries almost everyone would categorize as large libraries and library systems. The Salt Lake City Public Library serves 183,171 people in Utah from half a dozen locations. Its Twitter account had 1,500 followers as of December 2011, while its Facebook page showed 5,561 likes (3%). The two feeds have similar but not identical content. The last of the four Facebook updates below is mirrored by a tweet suggesting that people visit the Facebook page:

> If you couldn't make it to the one-on-one computer help session last week we're doing it again today at Main 4–6 P.M. **[Link] 2 people like this.**

> New stuff hits our shelves every day! Follow this link to check out lists + place holds on of all of our new material: **[Link]**

> Drop by the Sprague branch today between 2–4 P.M. to get one-on-one computer help from City Library experts: **[Link]**

> We've rededicated ourselves to providing short+timely messages to our followers on Twitter. If you don't already follow us, hop the link below and join the conversation! **[Link]**

Two libraries in this size category reach more than 2% of their potential patrons through Twitter. Kansas City Public Library in Missouri served nearly 240,000 people and had 6,105 followers (2.5%) as of December 13, 2011. The following five tweets were all on the day I checked the account:

> Good coffee = better reading. RT @lifehacker: Give your coffee exotic flavors by infusing the beans with spices: **[Link]**

> Is time travel real only in storybooks? Interesting take on H.G. Wells vs. science, via @bigthink. **[Link]**

> Even teen celebs aren't immune to bullies. YouTube sensation Rebecca Black quits middle school (@mashable): **[Link]**

> We'll make something of you yet! RT @mbbagency: MBB excited to be signed up for the Big Read @KCLibrary. We be doin' sum learnin' #bigreadkc

> That's great! RT @jldobson: . . . We've got eleven readers signed up for the Big Read at @mbbagency. Can't wait to get started! #bigreadkc

The West Palm Beach Public Library in Florida serves just over 103,000 people. On December 6, 2011, its Twitter account had 2,396 followers (2.3%), and the most recent five tweets were all from the day checked. (The account seemed "bursty," with bunches of tweets on one day followed by several days without tweets.) When checked again on January 2, 2012, another 67 followers were on board! Examples from late December 2011 include:

> We're so thrilled to have Jacqueline Whitmore visiting the library to discuss her book! Thursday, January 12th at . . . [Link]

> Great @pbpost article on @etiquetteexpert Jacqueline Whitmore! She'll be speaking at the library on Thurs. 1/12. [Link]

> Morning peeps! Today we have Pilates at 10:30am & Latin Cardio at 6:00pm. Good way to burn off the holiday lbs!

> Love free stuff? Love saving the planet? Stop by the City's Office of Sustainability table at the Northwood . . . [Link]

Going north of the border, one of the responses to my query regarding social networks came from Ann Foster, branch supervisor at the Alice Turner Library, part of Saskatoon Public Library in Saskatchewan, Canada. The library's eight locations serve some 232,000 people. Here's what Foster had to say about the operation of the library's Twitter account (479 followers) and Facebook page (535 likes), both updated fairly frequently with sometimes-overlapping, sometimes-different content:

> We've been maintaining both a Facebook and a Twitter page for about a year now. I'm the chair of the Facebook/Twitter committee, and as such, I spend probably about 2 hours a week updating our pages and monitoring activity. We always try and respond to all of our comments on both platforms. The committee comprises 5 librarians as well as one member from our community relations (marketing) department. We've had great feedback about both pages, and our patrons seem to be using and liking both. In our area, Facebook is more popular than Twitter. We use the Facebook page to post events, short book lists, and library announcements and news. The Twitter feed is synched with the Facebook page so it posts everything we put on Facebook. We also include links to interesting articles and retweets on the Twitter feed (after learning early on that too much posting in the Facebook page was off-putting to patrons. Twitter users seem more patient with lots of updates)

These five tweets all came on the same day:

> Annabelle Hepburn: #yxe please RT: FLASH MOB FIGHTING POVERTY! There will be a flashmob in @ the CTV studio @ 12.29pm TODAY! Spread the word, peeps . . .

Heard a good book lately? Pick up some book CDs from our extensive collection in Fine Arts on the second floor of . . . [Link]

#FF amazing #yxe nonprofit tweeps [list of Twitter names]

@VictorDas All of our events are listed in Library News magazine, we're working on getting an online calender too! [Link]

RT @weyburnpublic: Do you know any piano playing afficianadoes? Because the library piano in the basement has been awfully lonely lately.

These three Facebook updates arrived over a two-day period:

Heard a good book lately? Pick up some book CDs from our extensive collection in Fine Arts on the second floor of the Frances Morrison Library downtown. Some new titles to try—The Peach Keeper by Sarah Addison Allen, or Our Man in Tehran by Robert Wright. Do you have any other recommendations worth listening to?

Children's book too hot for U.S. publishers warmly received in Canada [Link]

Please join SPL tonight for a talk and discussion on Animal Contributions to Society. Animal Contributions to Society Location: Frances Morrison Library / Theatre / Lower Level Time: 7:00PM Thursday, September 15th

Are these accounts reaching a huge percentage of the service population? No—but they're reaching enough people, effectively enough, to justify two hours a week updating and monitoring them. Note Foster's key sentence: "We always try and respond to all of our comments on both platforms."

LIBRARIES SERVING 250,000 TO 499,000 PEOPLE

Live Oak Public Libraries in Georgia serves some 338,000 people, 4,608 of whom (1.4%) like its Facebook account (which averages about one post per day). The following examples have been trimmed:

It's Elvis Week (Aug. 10–16)! Celebrate by checking out his music CDs, reading a book about him, or enjoying his movies on DVD. Our film pick is 1961's "Blue Hawaii" . . . so fun! **Alissa likes this.**

> **Chad** This movie is the reason I was named Chad. . . .

> **Live Oak Public Libraries** And that must be why you're the "King" of Summer Reading, Chad! :) Thanks for a great job this summer—everyone enjoyed your shows!

> **Chad** Thank you, thank you very much. :)

Only 8 days to go! Our 2011 Summer Reading Program ends August 19, so make sure you turn in those Reading Logs! Info @ **[Link]** You could have a chance to win some awesome prizes, like a two night family stay at the Hyatt Regency Atlanta plus tickets for two adults and two children to major Atlanta attractions. Dolphin Tales show at the Georgia Aquarium, anyone? :) **[Link] Alissa likes this.**

Perhaps it's worth noting that the interchange in the first post took place over a two-hour period.

Richland County Public Library in South Carolina serves more than 320,000 people and had 4,140 likes (1.3%) for its Facebook account, which would seem to average at least one post per day. Examples include the following:

Have you downloaded your 3 songs this week? #freemusic at **[Link] 10 people like this.**

> **Crystal** Yes! I almost forgot :)

> **Sherry** Wow!

> **Debra** Thanks for the reminder!

Looking for something to do with the kids in the morning? Check out storytimes happening at several locations. **[Link] Jennifer Crossman likes this.**

> **Alicia** Will "Hola, Libros" be a regular event? I noticed it only once on the August calendar and then once in September, but on a Saturday instead of Monday. Sounds exciting! We plan to be there this Monday. **Saturday at 8:39pm**

LIBRARIES SERVING 500,000 OR MORE PEOPLE

Most very large libraries didn't have high percentages of followers or likes—about 0.3% for Facebook and 0.2% for Twitter on average. That's hardly surprising. There *were* five very large libraries where at least 1% of the community likes the Facebook page, one exceeding 2.5%. Let's look at the top three.

Columbus Metropolitan Library in Ohio serves more than 840,000 people. Its Facebook page had more than 22,000 likes in early November 2011 (2.6%) and its Twitter account more than 7,300 followers (not quite 1%). The Facebook page averaged around an update a day, including this sampling:

> Staff Pick Friday. Read Nancy's review of The Ecstasy of Defeat by the editors of The Onion. Ridiculously perfect. Sports interest not even required. I mean, nonstop brilliance in cadence and comedy everything. Here's a randomly picked example: Shaun White's profile blurb: "Accolades: Dew Tour medals in vert, superpipe, slopestyle, superslope, vertstyle, slopepipe, styliestyle, and superstyle vert pipe." **Angel likes this.**

> Outstanding First Novels of 2011 It's been a banner year for fiction debuts! While it can be exciting to read someone new, it's even more thrilling to discover a new author at the launch of their writing career. Donna Seaman of Booklist sums up the appeal when she wrote, "We celebrate first novels . . .

Multnomah County Library in Oregon serves more than 720,000 people. While its Twitter account certainly had lots of followers (3,831 in mid-December 2011, with more than 500 added over four months) and was *very* active (the most recent 20 tweets were over a three-day period), the Facebook account had a much larger following: 15,655 likes, or just under 2.2% of the population, for a page that averaged just under one update per day. Here are two Facebook updates from Multnomah with some text omitted:

> We're coming down to the wire, folks. The end of Adult Summer Reading is near. You have until August 31 to fill out and return your Read 4 Life cards (available at all locations). When you do, you are entered into a drawing for an e-book reader or a pair of season tickets to Literary Arts. How fab is that? **[Link] 15 people like this.**

>> **Rachel** Ah shoot. I didn't realize that audiobook counted. I listen to them all of the time! (Not much time for sit-down reading as I'm a very busy mom.)

>> **Kate** @Belinda, it's not too late. You have until Aug. 31. Just pick up and fill out a card by then.

What's your superpower? So you've got a metal skeleton and healing factor . . . but can you make history exciting, bub? Come chat with Portland Mercury reporter and zine author Sarah Mirk about comics, zines and little-known stories from our state and city's history **[Link] 9 people like this.**

Anthony This is my new favorite photo. **Tuesday at 6:40pm**

Another very large Pacific Northwest library, Seattle Public Library, serves more than 600,000 people—and while it had 1,595 followers for its Twitter account (averaging around two tweets per day), the Facebook account (just under two posts per day) had 12,646 likes as of early December 2011, 2% of the population (some 1,000 of those were added in four months). Here are two Facebook updates from Seattle (some text omitted):

On Thursday we asked you about your favorite cooking memoirs; you came up with some great options—here's the list! **[Link] 7 people like this.**

Laurel Fabulous. It's not exactly food, but also a shout out for *Love by the Glass* by Gaiter and Brecher, a love story told through wine.

Did you know that four of the 2011 winners of the World Beard Championships are from Washington state? Marvelous mustaches, beautiful beards! **[Link] David and 22 others like this.**

Walt Is there a world championship for bald guys? If so, I suspect Seattle's in the running for that as well.

Olympic Hot Tub Company Oh my . . .

I noticed two things immediately about both sets of updates: a fair amount of community engagement and a personal voice and informal tone, despite the sheer size of these libraries.

· It Takes All Sizes ·

There are vivid, highly engaged social network presences in libraries of all sizes, along with quite a few that are neither so engaged nor so active. I believe most public libraries are succeeding with social networking to some extent—and that most of them can, and would like to, do even better. The next two chapters look more closely at each social network.

....

CHAPTER 4

FACEBOOK SUCCESS AND STRATEGIES

DOES YOUR LIBRARY use Facebook effectively? Could your Facebook page be more effective than it is? Only you and your community can answer the first question. In most cases, I'd suggest that the answer to the second question would be that yes, most library Facebook pages could be more effective than they are.

Hard-core business types would probably redefine "effective" as "having high ROI," or return on investment. They'd urge you to make sure every hour spent updating and monitoring Facebook yielded the highest possible return and compare your ROI on Facebook to what you could get elsewhere.

The problem is that, at least partly, public libraries are not businesses. They're community institutions, and effectiveness must be measured against the needs and desires of the community.

I can't measure your effectiveness externally (any more than the two national library rankings can claim to be objectively meaningful in terms of community satisfaction and engagement). I can offer a variety of perspectives and notes on what other libraries (and perhaps your own) were actually doing in late 2011.

·Does Your Library Have a Facebook Page?·

The first question is the simplest: Does your library have a Facebook page, and is it, in fact, your page? Here's what I found in late 2011 when looking for Facebook pages for libraries—first on the library's home page (if it existed), next within the first 100 results on Facebook, and finally within Facebook itself:

- For 1,882 libraries (31.6%), I found a Facebook link of some sort on the library home page.
- For 1,306 libraries (21.9%), I found a Facebook page through Google, a page that clearly belonged to the library.
- For 20 libraries (0.3%), I found a Facebook page that clearly belonged to the library by searching directly within Facebook.
- For 1,050 libraries (17.6%), I found a Facebook page through Google—but it was a Community Page or autogenerated page from Wikipedia, not a page controlled by the library. I'd guess there are at least another 1,000 of these among the 3,210 libraries for which I found library-controlled Facebook pages, since a real page always took priority over a Community Page.
- Finally, for 1,700 libraries (28.5%), I was unable to find a Facebook page at all.
- So you could claim that 71.5% of the libraries show up on Facebook—not including thousands of cases where library-related pages show up that are clearly under somebody else's control—but the appropriate figure is that already given in chapter 3: 3,208, or 53.8% of the 5,958 libraries. That figure includes the 11% of Facebook pages that are either moribund or too new to measure properly, and most of these are defunct or moribund.

DEALING WITH YOUR FACEBOOK PAGE(S)

If you've carried out the social networking audit recommended in chapter 2, you should know what Facebook page or pages exist for your library. Even if your library doesn't currently plan to use Facebook, it makes sense to see whether you have a page—and, if so, what you can do about it or with it.

If you find one or more Community Pages when you search for your library, you should be able to claim them—and to merge up to five of them into an authenticated page that your library controls. According to Nick O'Neill's November 8, 2010, article at *allfacebook*, "Facebook Now Letting Brands Claim Community Pages":

> All you need to do is visit a community Page that has used your brand name and click on the link at the bottom which states "Is This Your Page?" After clicking, you will be brought through a verification process to confirm that you are truly the owner of the Page.[1]

O'Neill quotes from a Facebook help page that disappeared before he posted this article:

> Once you have submitted the request to merge the Community Page(s) to your authenticated Page, Facebook will review your request and verify that the merge request is for two similar entities. For example, the Community Page for Nike could merge with the authenticated Nike Page, but a merge request for Nike Basketball or Nike Shoes to merge to the general Nike Page would not be approved.
>
> Please keep in mind that the review process may take a few days, and that we may contact you if we need additional information. If we approve the request, anyone who has "Liked" the Community Page(s) will be combined and connected to your authenticated Page.

While it's apparently possible to gain control over these Community Pages, your library must take action: It won't happen automatically. When I asked for feedback on social networks from libraries, the blog post was automatically posted to FriendFeed, where I received a number of indirect comments. One of the commenters offered this paraphrased note about his public library (where he doesn't work):

> Sadly, as far as I can tell, our public library here does not make use of any social media. . . . Oops, stand corrected. They apparently have an FB page, found by searching in FB. It is not linked in any way to their main website. And it appears that no one is taking care of it. Just basic info, no news or feed. So, they may as well not have it. [2]

Neither the city nor the commenter's name is important here, as this could be true of hundreds of different places. Checking, I found that this was indeed a Community Page; other than the address and phone number of the library, there's nothing there but listings for six "nearby places" (all but one of them businesses) and the following disclaimer: "Community Pages are not affiliated with, or endorsed by, anyone associated with the topic."

In other words, the library does not have it—that page is not affiliated with the library itself. During this survey, I consistently found that Community Pages did not show up in Facebook searches, but they did in Google searches. In any case, your library should claim such pages, which you can apparently do only after you've established and authenticated your own library page.

· Motivations and Methods ·

If you're just starting a Facebook page, the relevant question may be, What do you plan for the Facebook page? If you already have one, there are two more relevant questions: How is it being used? Is that the best use?

"Best" is another one of those loaded terms. A use isn't the best use if it isn't feasible or sustainable, and what's best for Multnomah County, Oregon (serving more than 700,000 people), may not be what's best for Homer, Alaska (serving some 5,000 people).

Claudia Hanes comments on the situation in Homer and on why that library doesn't (yet) use Twitter:

> Our library uses Facebook. We have two pages—one directed at the general Homer Public Library community and the other directed at the teen community.
>
> Facebook posts are considered part of our publicity strategy for programs and an effective way to communicate timely messages to the public. For each post, approximately 15 minutes is required to develop the post and submit it. Most posts follow a similar structure. Occasionally, links to other information sources are shared, but these require a minimal amount of time. Most of these postings are a result of the Facebook administrators seeing the noteworthy item on their own and then identifying the relevancy for the Homer Public Library community.
>
> Four people are the administrators for the pages. The general feedback from users has been positive. Over 500 people receive our postings. Limited numbers respond to the postings directly, but many use it as an information source. While I personally use Twitter, I don't think it would be an effective tool for our library. To use it effectively requires more staff time.

Homer's main Facebook page shows reasonable activity for a small library (more than one post per week) and quite a bit of community engagement. Following are four posts from a three-day period in late October 2011:

> 'Tis the season for horror! Check out our horror-ific books for teens and adults on display at the library! **[Wall Photos]**
>
> **Paula** Who is the HPL fb master!??? You are doing a great job!!!!
>
> **Homer Public Library** Claudia, Holly, and Teresa are the HPL Facebook admins. Thanks, Paula!

> Just in time for Halloween- a FACE PAINTING workshop! There's no school on Thursday (10/27), so join us at the library from 1–3pm for tips and ideas to help your costume! The FREE workshop is for ages 11 and up. Supplies provided. **[Wall Photos] 2 people like this.**

> Are you under 18? Scared of the fines on your juvenile library card? Stop by HPL this week (today through Sat. 10/29) and have those late fees forgiven! For anyone under 18 only! **[Wall Photos]**

> Job announcement: FHL Coordinator The Friends of the Homer Public Library is seeking an energetic and organized individual to assist the FHL board with office administration, implementing programs, coordinating volunteers and fundraising activities. A complete job description is available at the library. **Laura Watson likes this.**

Each post requires a quarter-hour to create and additional time to respond to comments—and the items reach 11% of the community. It would be hard to describe this as anything less than effective.

When I first worked on this chapter, after the initial scan of 25 states, I said this: "As it happens, as of summer 2011, *no* Alaska public library appears to use Twitter." But when I revisited the libraries four months later, I found three—two of them clearly very new, with 15 and 33 tweets, respectively, and one I might have failed to find in August. One of those three is even smaller than Homer, serving just under 2,700 people—Seward Community Library. The Twitter account was not reaching many people (it had three followers as of early January 2012), but it was active, as in these four tweets from a one-week period in December 2011:

> A komodo dragon has been spotted @SewardLibrary! Kids from 1–92 will want to stop by during the holidays to see this bionical wonder!

> Check out Bits of History—William H. Seward School **[Link]**
> #bitsofhistory #Seward

Give yourself a break and grab a light read. We've got a variety of books on display to help you escape. [Link]

In case you stopped by between 5:30–6, you'll notice we closed early due to power outage. Stop by tomorrow when we're up & running again!

Interestingly, especially for such a small library, Seward's Facebook page (which is more active and has 79 likes, 3% of the community) has almost entirely different content. From the same week:

Seward Community Library shared a link. Bits of History—William H. Seward School [Link] In this "Gone But Not Forgotten" segment, learn about the history of the Seward school on Fourth Avenue in Seward, AK.

Christmas Story Time!—at Seward Community Library. [Event]

---

14 Wish Tree sponsors and counting! [Photo] 2 people like this.

Power outages are always a great time to slow down . . . and read (flashlight sold separately). 4 people like this.

Elly If only my Kindle had a backlight.

Marie Spratlin Hasskarl, director at Connecticut's Burlington Public Library, comments on their process:

We had a volunteer set us up and post items for us for about two years then she got busy searching for a job so the staff took over. We post programs primarily but from time to time we might post other bits of information that are library or literary related. We have had people call us about programs they have seen posted to ask more questions. *We love Facebook and I think this is another way to reach people and the response has been positive.* We also post library pictures there from time to time. [Emphasis added]

Burlington's Facebook page has 248 likes in a community of some 9,000 people (2.7%) and seems to average at least two updates a week. Here are four examples from the first two weeks of August 2011:

Tonight Tuesday, Aug 16 @ 6:30 pm—A World of Stories with "Transformations," All ages. Storytelling and painted faces combine in this unique performance of traditional folk tales. Let's celebrate a great summer of reading! [Wall Photos]

Tonight is Tween/Teen craft night, and we are making magnetic locker tins to keep things organized in a fun and decorative way this fall!!! Bring tins from Altoids, Eclipse mints, band-aids, Sucrets or others and get creative!

August 9 African Drumming with Downright Music of Collinsville, All ages. Learn about African drumming at this interactive event where we will learn how drums are made, their history, and how to use them! **[Wall Photos] Brenda Thackaberry likes this.**

Thursday night Tween/Teen craft—BANDLETS. If you don't know what they are, come in and find out!

Going to an even smaller community, here's part of what Carrie Andrew had to say about Facebook at Norwood Public Library in Colorado:

> Our library has only had a Facebook page for the last 11 months. I created it once I became director and am the only one who has administrative rights on the page, not because I am a control freak but because I am one of two full time employees in a very small district.... Being a small, rural, ranching community the average level of technological competence is quite low due to lack of exposure.... Facebook is about the only means of getting up to date local info, through people's status updates, because we don't have a radio station and only a weekly newspaper.
>
> I have used Facebook to create events for things that are happening at the library so that I can send out invites to everyone. We recently had a local author in to sell and sign copies of her recent book. I only advertised through Facebook events the day before but we ended up with 13 attendees which we considered to be quite good. Several of them said they had heard about it only through Facebook. I've also used it quite a bit this summer posting photos of our various events for the summer reading programs....
>
> I feel that people are beginning to know and use our page to find out about programming and often have people send me chat messages or wall posts with library questions of one type or another.

The Norwood Public Library Facebook page (there's also a teen page) had 160 likes in December 2011 in a community of fewer than 2,000 people: 8% of the community. Andrew raises an excellent point: In many smaller communities, Facebook might be the only way to get current information out to the community—and in some larger ones it may be one of the best and easiest.

Following are updates from late September and early October 2011 showing distinctly strong community engagement:

Norwood Public Library added 27 new photos to the album Our Library and Staff. **6 people like this.**

> **Trish** Great photos! Everything looks so nice and neat!

> **Coleen** I love my library!

> **Becky** You are doing such a wonderful job, congratulations!

> **Carolyn** Testament of what a great job you girls are doing! Thanks for all the hard work you put in to making our library such a great place to visit!

> **Norwood Public Library** Thank you all for your encouragement!!

Our library eBooks are now compatible with Kindle® and Kindle® reading apps!

The Library Book Sale is in full swing! We'll be open tomorrow too so stop by before or after the parade! **Francis N Carolann likes this.**

> **Becky** I hope it goes really well!

Finally (for this set of examples), consider Boulder City Library, serving some 16,000 people in Nevada. Lynn Schofield-Dahl, the director, offered a range of comments, a few of which are excerpted here:

> We use Facebook primarily as an online newsletter, sending out news concerning special events at the library, closures, computer classes, job openings, etc. While we have a rather small group of "friends," other local businesses have "liked" us, and our status appears on their pages as well.
>
> The greatest impact I have seen from using FB has been an increase in attendance at programs. I'm especially happy to note an increase of attendance at our programs targeting adults. We have also had some luck in using FB to poll the public, though we still get greater response from in-house surveys.
>
> On the applications for the last 2 job openings we had . . . several people noted they learned of the positions via FB.
>
> I spend very little time each week at FB for the library. Each Monday Morning I post a list of events for the week. A couple of times a month, I spend an afternoon posting upcoming events. When we have some good photos to share, I post those in our photo albums. *Maybe twice a day I check the page to see if we have any comments from readers to which I need to respond.* It is rare that I have posts to which I feel the need to respond. [Emphasis added]

The Facebook page shows 141 likes, less than 1% of the community—but maybe that's enough in this case. Skimming through recent updates shows a significant number of community questions—with rapid, down-to-earth responses from the library as appropriate.

GAINING INSIGHTS INTO HOW IT'S GOING

While your library should have some general plan for Facebook or Twitter use before starting a page or account, that plan should be a starting point, not a rigid framework. A living social network account will change over time for any number of good reasons.

One thing you should do, at least once in a while, is to see how things are going. From outside, all I can see is how many likes you have and what's actually happening on your page, but from inside you can gather a lot more information.

Facebook Page Insights provides fairly extensive information on the performance of your page. Start with "About Facebook Insights" in the Facebook Help Center, download *Facebook Page Insights: Product Guide for Facebook Page Owners*, and proceed from there.[3] The service is free, and your library should take advantage of it.

FROM HOW TO WHY

It's one thing to determine how your library will use Facebook and other social networks, a determination that must be kept flexible as you see what works and your community responds. It's another to consider the *why*: your library's primary motivation for its social network.

Brian Mathews addressed this issue in "Why Does My Library Use Social Media?" posted July 6, 2011, at *The Ubiquitous Librarian.* The post follows a talk Mathews gave for LLAMA during the ALA 2011 Annual Conference in New Orleans. While Mathews was an AUL (Assistant University Librarian) at the time and is now an assistant dean in a university library (formerly UCSB, now Virginia Tech), this is a case where what he says may apply equally well to most public libraries.

He notes the responses you're likely to get when you ask librarians why they're involved with social networks. Following are some of those responses (excluding one that's fairly specific to educational institutions):

- To promote library services, workshops, and events
- To provide better access to information
- To be where the users are
- To collect feedback from patrons[4]

To Mathews, these are "what we are doing, not why we are doing it." He's proposing an answer to the latter question for his own library:

> Our purpose—the reason why we use the social web is to find people who "like" the library and give them a way to express it. We will use this platform to nurture that bond and move them from like to love. [Develop their passion.] We also want to enable them to share this experience and help bring others into this relationship.[5]

He's looking to develop "a small focused niche audience" rather than necessarily being where his community is—he wants to treat fans or followers as VIPs, getting them more engaged.

Does his answer work for your library? Should you consider it? I'm not recommending Mathews's "why" as one that should apply everywhere. But it's worth thinking past the *what* and considering the *why*. That's particularly true for larger libraries, where the chances of having a large percentage of the community liking your Facebook page are fairly slender. Maybe the large percentage isn't necessary?

· The Sobering Reality of Reach ·

This may be the best place to introduce a table that could be used by someone dismissive of social networks as evidence that they're useless for public libraries—to wit, the actual numbers of followers and percentages of those who could plausibly follow library Facebook pages. Before you look at table 4.1, reread the previous paragraph, specifically these two sentences: "But it's worth thinking past the *what* and considering the *why*. That's particularly true for larger libraries, where the chances of having a large percentage of the community liking your Facebook page are fairly slender."

For table 4.1, the *Population* column includes only those libraries that have Facebook pages. The numbers here are pretty stark. If you're a glass-half-empty sort, you could say that nearly 99.5% of library patrons who could like their library's Facebook pages don't—and for the largest libraries, that rises to 99.7%. That's factual, but I don't think it's the relevant truth. I believe it's more relevant that nearly a million library users do like their library's Facebook pages, an act that exposes those users to a stream of library data. What's also interesting here

TABLE 4.1

Likes for library Facebook pages

SIZE	POPULATION	LIKES	LIKE%
H0	76,640	6,832	8.91%
H1	492,917	20,934	4.25%
H2	1,368,816	36,217	2.65%
H3	3,940,255	72,300	1.83%
H4	12,698,161	148,367	1.17%
H5	16,517,371	140,515	0.85%
H6	20,942,256	119,971	0.57%
H7	34,929,788	154,609	0.44%
H8	27,148,437	96,834	0.36%
H9	71,055,399	202,358	0.28%
TOTAL	**189,170,040**	**998,937**	**0.53%**
Rural	18,576,789	284,650	1.53%
Urban	170,593,251	714,287	0.42%
Small	5,878,628	136,283	2.32%
Medium	50,157,788	408,853	0.82%
Large	133,133,624	453,801	0.34%

is that the steady change seen in most library-size tables is neatly reversed. Look back at figure 3.1 (p. 30) and compare it to figure 4.1.

Those are overall percentages to be sure. Many libraries do much better. We'll look at some of those examples and some other relevant figures later in this chapter, but for now let's consider some other comments on Facebook and other social networking practices.

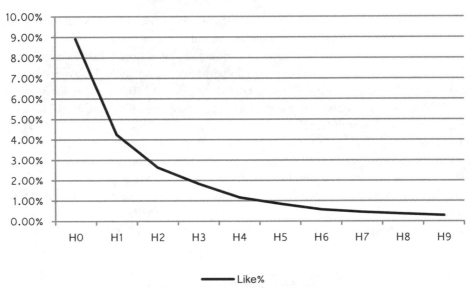

FIGURE 4.1

Like as percentage of LSA population

· Social Networking Best Practices ·

That's the title for Miss Information's list of best practices based on her experience at a "busy suburban library" and recounted on the *Closed Stacks* blog in a March 14, 2011, post (lightly excerpted):

> When I first entered library school, Librarian About Town's innovative Myspace page for her community college library was getting recognized on a national level. No one was using social networking as a promotional or engagement tool for their library yet, and my friend was ahead of the pack.
>
> Just a few years later, almost all libraries have Facebook pages, and we are figuring out as a profession just how we'd like to use them. Are we engaging with our community on these pages, asking for feedback? Are we promoting programs? What exactly are these pages for?
>
> Recently, I took over my library's Facebook page and found myself just regurgitating the information I had posted on our website. I could see why posting the information to Facebook was useful—not everyone goes to our library's website every day, but I knew as a Facebook user, I would be awfully bored with what I was posting as my library.
>
> [A friend offered "really innovative and useful" principles:]

Have a personality: Don't just post on topics about your library. Post any information you think your patrons might be interested in. . . .

Ask questions, interact: Social media is new and innovative because it is social. As librarians we are always looking for ways to solicit feedback from our patrons. . . .

Act like a person: Facebook now allows you to respond to your library's friends' posts as the library . . . respond to your Facebook friend's updates and comments. Tell them you loved that book too! That will keep your library's name out there, and engage more patrons/fans.

Make your followers feel like the in-crowd: Did you just get in a big shipment of romance novels? Tell Facebook first. . . .

Keep an eye on what the most people interact with: This one is obvious, keep doing what works. If lots of people loved hearing about Lucy the Read Dog, post about other similar children's programs. . . .

Expand: I don't just have a library Facebook. I have a Facebook, a Foursquare, a Gowalla, a newspaper column, a local cable television show . . . I am covering my bases. I want my patrons to know what's happening and use our services and I will get to them somehow![6]

By now, you know that "almost all libraries have Facebook pages" is misinformation. I'm also not sure expanding makes sense for smaller libraries, and there are equity issues with targeting specific patrons' interests only on Facebook (e.g., active library users who detest Facebook). That said, this is an interesting set of practices to consider.

On the other hand, you have to consider that if you ask questions and get few responses—or none at all—does that mean you're failing? As I've looked at thousands of Facebook updates, including scores of outright questions, I rarely see more than two or three responses even on pages with thousands of likes.

As you ponder the suggestions above, you might also read "How Facebook Can Help Market Your Library," posted on the blog of the Tampa Bay Library Consortium on January 6, 2012.[7] This brief discussion notes some benefits of a library page, some "great perks" (e.g., sharing information for free, answering patron questions, or getting feedback), and some ideas for improving activity on an existing page. Following are more examples:

- Add a social media button to your website and blog.
- Add a Facebook link to your e-mail signature (easy promotion every time you send an e-mail).
- Post pictures from classes in the library or reading club. Make sure to tag and share them, with patrons' permission, and then their friends who don't know about your page will "like" your page.

FAILURE TO FOLLOW

As a library patron, I'd be delighted to see the occasional pertinent, useful, interesting question, just as I'd be delighted to see prompt library responses if I have a comment or question.

Maybe this needs to be stressed, as I'd consider it the most significant failure in some (fortunately, not most) library Facebook pages—to wit, there are pages where patrons ask questions and never get responses.

If you have a Facebook page or Twitter account, *somebody* from the library with the authority to reply to comments needs to check it at least once a day, at least on days that you're open. Nothing will shut down community engagement faster than the feeling that followers are talking to a brick wall.

LAURA SOLOMON ON BEING TRANSPARENT

I'll quote very selectively from Laura Solomon's *Doing Social Media So It Matters* one more time—the topic headings for her section "Being Transparent" in the chapter "Strategies for Media Success":[8]

- Find your library's voice
- Talk about the challenges of your library
- Explain changes
- Own up to your mistakes
- Talk about individual staff

While these suggestions don't deal with overall methods for doing effective Facebook posts (read her book for more in that area), they offer excellent advice on transparency and honesty, critical to making your wall more than just a list of events and hours.

"Own up to your mistakes" works at the smallest level as well as the largest. I've seen typos and grammatical errors in Facebook updates from libraries of all sizes. They happen. They especially happen when your library encourages informal posts rather than a strictly PR-level tone. If your community is actively engaged with the library, somebody will point out the errors. If that happens and there's an *appropriate*, cheerful response (frequently beginning with "Oops!" or an equivalent note), the mistake becomes an accidental positive—as long as your Facebook wall isn't full of such mistakes. If someone points out an error and is met with silence from your end, you're establishing the library's nonresponsive attitude toward social networking and thoughtful patrons will soon stop trying.

Am I saying that even a library serving more than a million people should show personalities within its Facebook wall? I am indeed.

· Other Voices ·

A number of librarians responded to my query on social network usage but preferred not to be quoted by name. One director of a library serving fewer than 1,000 people notes "I haven't had many responses—maybe three in the last two years" and lately "haven't spent much time at it with no one looking at it," noting that the town has "a lot of older residents who are not computer literate." (The page has likes from 2% of the community, but that's not a large actual number.) Another, from a similarly small community, says there's "good feedback but wish it were more. It will take awhile to catch on in our community." That page shows a high percentage of likes (over 8% of the community in late October 2011), and a recent check of updates shows good activity and a fair amount of feedback. It seems to be catching on.

One background commenter from a community of 1,000 people where 9% like the Facebook page says that three people on the small staff post events, taking about an hour a week total, for one simple reason: "We use Facebook because a number of our patrons use it. It is a good way to get the word out to that segment of our population."

Finally, one person from a *very* small library (under 400 with a dozen likes on its Facebook page), who was willing to be quoted but whom I'll use as background, wonders whether it's worth it in this particular case. The person was told by three book club members that they found out about the book club from Facebook, but updates "take too much time" for a person who's frequently the only staff member. "I don't have a half hour or 15 minutes to spare sometimes. I have other priorities." Checking in at that library's Facebook page in late October 2011, it was now up to 16 likes (more than 4% of the community), and while there aren't lots of posts, the posts are personal, informative, and engaging. (This library is open 32 hours a week, which seems little short of astonishing for a community that small.)

A FEW DATA POINTS ON FACEBOOK FOCUS AND CONVERSATION

Looking at the five most recent updates (when I was surveying the initial 25 states, primarily in late July through August 2011), I found that 931 of the 1,158 Facebook accounts had some sign of community engagement. That's 80%, and while the engagement was frequently limited to explicitly liking a specific update or responding with something like "Great!" or "We'll be there!" it's still a remarkably positive indicator. Within that 80%, more than half (498 accounts, 43% of the total) had at least one comment from someone within the community, while 433 (37%) had at least one like but no comments. Note that those numbers were only for the most recent five updates as of when I checked a page. For libraries with frequent updates, comments might very well turn up a day or two later. Looking at more than 3,100 Facebook pages in 38 states later in 2011, I found that 90% had at least one comment or outside post, and almost all of the other 10% had at least one like on a post. At this point, very nearly all library Facebook pages have some conversation.

As for focus, most libraries cover a mix of topics—but there are some cases where, at least for a five-post snapshot, there is an apparent focus (when I've looked at longer streams, the foci seem to stay fairly consistent). Looking only at the summer 2011 survey, the largest cluster was Facebook pages focused almost entirely on events: 14%, with another 2.3% combining events and library services and hours. Just over 1% seemed to focus primarily on books, with less than ½% focusing on materials in general and a few focused on specific construction projects. More than 80% of the pages covered a variety of events, hours, services, and other topics.

A UNIVERSITY LIBRARY PERSPECTIVE

Chris Bourg is an AUL at Stanford University Libraries, and while this book focuses on public libraries, some of her comments about the Facebook page for Stanford's Green Library (in an August 22, 2011, post at *Feral Librarian*) are relevant to library Facebook usage in general. Following are excerpts from that post:

> We now have 2,846 people who Like us (up from 809 in July 2009, when I last reported our fan numbers); and I remain convinced that we are the most popular academic library on Facebook. . . . We have not done any paid Ads since summer

of 2008—all of our new Fans/Likes have been gained organically. . . . [Notes on the page's high level of comments and usage.]

I'm convinced that our success is based largely on the fact that we post interesting content, tailored to the interests of people who truly Like libraries. Most of what lands on our Facebook page is pulled automatically from our blog, but occasionally one of the Facebook admins will post something just to Facebook. The Facebook only posts are usually just quick links to outside articles of interest, often humorous (or intended to be humorous). . . .

For us, Facebook provides an extra venue for interacting with people who Like us; and the small amount of effort dedicated to keeping it up to date is certainly worth it.[9]

How does a Facebook page get to have big numbers? To me, the last two paragraphs make complete sense, for Stanford and for most public libraries.

· Numbers, Benchmarks, and Examples ·

Here are some benchmarks for Facebook reach and frequency, along with examples of libraries and some names of libraries whose Facebook pages you might wish to look at.

TABLE 4.2

The Facebook matrix: Facebook pages, by reach/frequency code

	a	b	c	d	e	TOTAL
1	55	136	198	192	75	656
2	29	89	183	222	89	612
3	19	87	184	278	146	714
4	28	41	112	221	162	564
5	8	16	50	87	90	251
6	4	14	32	76	218	344
TOTAL	143	383	759	1,076	780	3,141

Table 4.2 shows the Facebook pages for which I could readily assign reach/frequency codes and the number of libraries for each code. For example, 656 pages have very frequent updates, with 55 of those pages having very broad reach; at the other extreme, 218 pages were both new or moribund and have limited reach. Table 4.3 shows the same information, but as percentages.

I believe most libraries should aim for the upper left area—to have at least fairly wide reach (a–c) and reasonable activity (1–3). In practice, just over 31% of the libraries with Facebook pages, or just under 1,000, are already there.

Except for a few pages that are too new to measure properly, my sense is that most libraries in category 6, 11%, have essentially given up on Facebook. That leaves 58% of libraries that should have plenty of room for growth.

TABLE 4.3

Percentage of Facebook pages for each reach/frequency code

	a	b	c	d	e	TOTAL
1	1.8%	4.3%	6.3%	6.1%	2.4%	20.9%
2	0.9%	2.8%	5.8%	7.1%	2.8%	19.5%
3	0.6%	2.8%	5.9%	8.9%	4.6%	22.7%
4	0.9%	1.3%	3.6%	7.0%	5.2%	18.0%
5	0.3%	0.5%	1.6%	2.8%	2.9%	8.0%
6	0.1%	0.4%	1.0%	2.4%	6.9%	11.0%
TOTAL	4.6%	12.2%	24.2%	34.3%	24.8%	100.0%

DO EXTREMELY FREQUENT UPDATES MAKE SENSE?

When sampled in fall 2011, a surprising 41 library Facebook pages had at least five updates within 24 hours of the time I was checking them—in other words, five updates a day.

That strikes me as a lot, and as a patron I doubt that I'd follow a library with so many updates. So the question is, How are these libraries doing in terms of reach?

It's hard to say. Of the 41, three have very broad reach (a1), three more have broad reach (b1), and 12 have fairly broad reach (c1), or about 43% total. That leaves 16 with moderate reach (d1) and seven with limited reach (e1), or 56% of the 41. All six with broad or very broad reach are small libraries.

As a comparison, consider another 615 Facebook pages averaging at least five updates per week—very frequent updating, but not five per day. Fifty-two of them have very broad reach, 133 have broad reach, and 186 have fairly broad reach. That's 60% in total, leaving 176 with moderate reach and 68 with limited reach, or 40%.

More strikingly, only 15% of those with extremely frequent updates have broad or very broad reach—whereas 30% of those with slightly less frequent updates manage that level. I find that difference suggestive. Realistically, most libraries just aren't going to update Facebook that often; the 615 to 41 ratio of very frequent to extremely frequent updates, more than 15 to 1, offers the real-world answer.

SHOULD VERY SMALL LIBRARIES AIM FOR DAILY UPDATES?

Five libraries serving fewer than 1,000 people seem to manage daily updates, although that may not be true over a longer period. I've already mentioned one of the five, Langdon Library in New Hampshire. Others include the Sullivan Public Library in New Hampshire, the Lied Randolph Public Library in Nebraska, the Hooper Public Library in Nebraska, and the Osceola Public Library in Nebraska.

Sullivan Public serves 796 people and has 89 likes (11%). The Facebook updates tend to be brief and varied, such as these from three days in December 2011:

> Sullivan Public Library shared a link. Some Books Saved by Egyptian Protestors at the Institut d'Egypte **[Link]**

> Sullivan Public Library shared a link. Wonderful Polish Christmas Tree Made from Books . . . & a How-To **[Link]**

> High school Students—Nominations are wanted for 2013. Flume Award **[Link]**

> Many choices in book formats these days **[Cartoon]**

Lied Randolph serves 816 with 283 likes (35%) and also has varied updates, such as these three from the same three days in December:

> Wow, 17 computers busy for the last two hours! Busy day! :) **3 people like this.**

> Kudos to the RHS Seniors who visited the library today . . . collectively, they donated close to 9000 grains of rice! **[Link] 2 people like this.**

> Ho, Ho, Ho, Christmas is almost here! Just a reminder that the library will be closed on Monday, December 26 and Monday, January 2 to celebrate the holidays. Wishing all our Facebook Friends many blessings and warm memories throughout the season! **Lisa likes this.**

A FEW EXAMPLES FROM THE UPPER LEFT SECTOR

Many of the libraries already used as examples fall into the upper left sector or use both Twitter and Facebook (and are discussed in chapter 5).

Pulaski County Public Library in Kentucky serves some 61,000 people from five locations and a bookmobile. Its Facebook account has more than 1,150 likes (1.9%) and offers moderately frequent updates. Here are examples from August 2011:

> Christian Fiction Author Jan Watson will be here Sept 10th to speak & sign copies of her books. She is the Author of the Troublesome Creek Series. Please call for more information.679-8401 **[Wall Photos]**

> New Coupon Swap and Forum on Saturday, August 20th at 1:00 P.M. Bring coupons and ideas to swap. **[Wall Photos] Charlotte likes this.**
>
>> **Pulaski County Public Library** This is going to be a monthly forum/swap. Bring a friend!!!

> Basic YOGA Class, Join Sherrye Tucker on Aug 17th at 10am to learn very basic Yoga! Bring Mat or Towel. **[Wall Photos]**
>
>> **Pulaski County Public Library** Had a wonderful turnout for Yoga this morning! Thank you Sherrye Tucker!!!!

The Essex Library Association in Connecticut serves fewer than 7,000 people. Its Facebook page has 373 likes (5.5%) and is updated every couple of days. Some examples from August 2011 are as follows:

> Novel Destinations; Linda has submitted a photo for extra points in our first adult summer reading program. (If you get a picture of yourself reading at a "novel destination," you get a bonus entry in the drawing for great prizes.) Want to play? Swing by and pick up an entry form, or download one from our website, read six adult books between now and the end of August, and you too can compete—for an e-reader or gift certificates from local merchants. Be in it to win it! **[Wall Photos] Jenny likes this.**

> Calling all Summer Readers! The End of Summer Reading Party is today! 3–5 P.M. at the Centerbrook Meeting House (51 Main St., Centerbrook) There will be Music! Food! Games! Crafts! Prizes! Come celebrate all the reading you've accomplished this summer! We're planning to have local band Binky help us celebrate and will be raffling off great door prizes. Come join the fun! **[Wall Photos] Jenny likes this.**

> Drop whatever you are doing this Thursday evening (August 18th) and come to the Essex Library to listen to author Mariana de Saint Phalle

along with Essex resident and illustrator Linda Woolcott talk about their book Mariana's Letters. These two delightful women have much to say about travel, cooking and living life well. 7 P.M. in the Program Room. Copies of the book will be available for purchase. Call 860 767-1560 for more information. **[Wall Photos] Jenny likes this.**

Paramus Public Library in New Jersey serves some 26,000 people from two locations. The Facebook page had 504 likes and about 20 updates per month, mostly event centered. Here are examples from early September 2011:

Don't forget! Today is Operation Goody Bag at the Library! Come and decorate a bag today! Until 8pm. **2 people like this.**

Tomorrow is the first day of school!! And the first day of TAB! Which one gives you yummy snacks, hmmm . . . ? Who's coming? Back to School TAB/Volunteer Meeting @ 2:45pm! Location: Paramus Public Library Time: 2:30PM **Mary likes this.**

Paramus Public Library created an event. Celebrate School! Wednesday, September 7, 2011 at 3:30pm

OTHER NUMBERS AND LIBRARIES YOU MIGHT WANT TO CHECK

Here, arranged by size of library, are the average and median reach of libraries (either percentage or number, depending on the size), the 80th percentile and 20th percentile, and a few of the library names with reach/frequency codes a1, a2, b1, and b2 that haven't already been mentioned and don't also have Twitter accounts. Most of these have Facebook links on the library's home page. In some cases, you may need to check the search results for the Facebook page.

H0: Libraries Serving Fewer Than 1,000 People
The average reach of the 115 Facebook pages in this category was 11.2%. The median was 5.2%. The 80th percentile was 13.3%—23 of the pages had that percentage or higher. The 20th was 1.7%—23 of the pages had that percentage or lower.

There were a few libraries in this group not already mentioned that combined strong activity and broad reach and that you might want to look at: Pawnee City Carnegie Public Library in Nebraska, Roger Clark Memorial Library in Vermont, Delta Community Library in Alaska, and Irene S. Sweetkind Public Library in New Mexico.

H1: Libraries Serving 1,000 to 2,499 People
The average reach of the 283 Facebook pages in this category was 4.6%. The median was 3.03%. The 80th percentile was 6.8%, and the 20th percentile was 1.1%.

A few more libraries in this group combined strong activity and broad reach (a few of *many*, showing no more than one per state): Cherryfield Free Public Library in Maine,

Williamsport-Washington Township Public Library in Indiana, Freedom Public Library in New Hampshire, Ouray Library District in Colorado, Milford Public Library in Utah, Mercer Public Library in Wisconsin, M. N. Spear Memorial Library in Massachusetts, Avalon Free Public Library in New Jersey, and Atglen Public Library in Pennsylvania.

H2: Libraries Serving 2,500 to 4,999 People

The average reach of the 370 Facebook pages in this category was 2.7%. The median was 2.0%. The 80th percentile was 4.3%. The 20th percentile was 0.8%.

A few more libraries in this group combined strong activity and broad reach: Bourbon Public Library in Indiana, Cook Memorial Library in New Hampshire, New York Mills Public Library in Minnesota, Marceline Carnegie Library in Missouri, Haines Borough Public Library in Alaska, Meekins Library in Massachusetts, Pittsfield Public Library in Maine, Bradford Public Library in Vermont, and Mineral County Public Library in Montana.

H3: Libraries Serving 5,000 to 9,999 People

The average reach of the 539 Facebook pages for libraries in this category was 1.9%. The median was 1.4%. The 80th percentile was 2.9%, and the 20th percentile was 0.6%.

A few libraries in this group combined strong activity and broad reach: Camden Public Library in Maine, Switzerland County Public Library in Indiana, Snake River School/Community Library in Idaho, Newcomerstown Public Library in Ohio, Cumberland County Public Library in Kentucky, Wetumpka Public Library in Alabama, and Durham Public Library in Connecticut.

H4: Libraries Serving 10,000 to 24,999 People

We're now moving into medium libraries, where my criteria for reach involved number of likes rather than percentage of potential patrons. For examples that follow (and in H5 and H6), "broad reach" means at least 500 likes rather than at least 5% (as in H0–H3).

The average reach among the 774 library Facebook pages in this group was 192. The median was 142. The 80th percentile was 290. The 20th percentile was 55.

Some libraries in this group combined strong activity and broad reach: Green County Public Library in Kentucky, Rio Grande City Public Library in Texas, Washington County Public Library in Alabama, Tipton County Public Library in Indiana, Twinsburg Public Library in Ohio, Newport Public Library in Oregon, Lakeville Public Library in Massachusetts, Kellogg-Hubbard Library in Vermont, and Hollidaysburg Area Public Library in Pennsylvania.

H5: Libraries Serving 25,000 to 49,999 People

The average reach among 469 Facebook pages in this group was 300. The median was 240. The 80th percentile was 447. The 20th percentile was 108.

Some libraries in this group had strong activity and broad reach: Hoover Public Library in Alabama, Scott County Public Library in Kentucky, Manheim Township Public Library in Pennsylvania, Hancock County Public Library in Indiana, Forbes Library in Massachusetts, Monterey Public Library in California, Beloit Public Library in Wisconsin, Winter Park Public Library in Florida, Uintah County Library in Utah, Coshocton Public Library in Ohio, and Talbot County Free Library in Maryland.

H6: Libraries Serving 50,000 to 99,999 People

The average reach among 293 Facebook pages in this group was 409. The median was 323. The 80th percentile was 653. The 20th percentile was 129.

Some libraries in this size range had strong activity and broad reach: Palos Verdes Library District in California, St. Mary's County Library in Maryland, Altoona Area Public Library in Pennsylvania, Carmel Clay Public Library in Indiana, Madison County Public Library in Kentucky, Pawtucket Public Library in Rhode Island, Old Bridge Public Library in New Jersey, St. Joseph Public Library in Missouri, Victoria Public Library in Texas, Roanoke Public Libraries in Virginia, Iberia Parish Library in Louisiana, and West Bend Community Memorial Library in Wisconsin.

H7: Libraries Serving 100,000 to 249,999 People

In this and the remaining two groups, the minimum number of likes for broad reach was 1,500. The average reach among 218 Facebook pages in this group was 422; the median was 427. The 80th percentile was 926, and the 20th percentile was 188.

Relatively few libraries in this size range had strong activity and broad reach, weren't already mentioned, and didn't also have Twitter. One example is Kitsap Regional Library in Washington.

H8: Libraries Serving 250,000 to 499,999 People

The average reach among 77 Facebook pages in this group was 1,258, with a median of 887. The 80th percentile was 2,230, and the 20th percentile was 256. Most libraries in this group were on both Twitter and Facebook; the single exception (not already mentioned) with broad reach and strong activity was Fort Vancouver Regional Library District in Washington.

H9: Libraries Serving 500,000 or More People

The average reach among the 70 Facebook pages in this group was 2,891, and the median was 1,545. The 80th percentile was 3,834, and the 20th percentile was 554. As with H8, most of the largest libraries were on both Twitter and Facebook. While there was one exception with strong activity and broad reach, a recheck in January 2012 found a Twitter account that was either new or had become findable.

NOTES

1. Nick O'Neill, "Facebook Now Letting Brands Claim Community Pages," *allfacebook*, November 8, 2010, http://allfacebook.com/facebook-notes-now-posting-large-images-in-feed_b22253.
2. Chris Bourg, "Update on Our Library Facebook Page," *Feral Librarian*, August 22, 2011.
3. Facebook, Inc., *Facebook Page Insights: Product Guide for Facebook Page Owners*, 2011, http://ads.ak .facebook.com/ads/FacebookAds/Page_Insights_en_US.pdf.
4. Brian Mathews, "Why Does My Library Use Social Media?" *The Ubiquitous Librarian*, July 6, 2011.
5. Ibid.
6. Miss Information, "Social Networking Best Practices," *Closed Stacks*, March 14, 2011, www.closed stacks.com/?p=3269.
7. "How Facebook Can Help Market Your Library," *Tampa Bay Library Consortium*, January 6, 2012, http://tblc.org/marketing/how-facebook-can-help-market-your-library.
8. Laura Solomon, *Doing Social Media So It Matters: A Librarian's Guide* (Chicago: American Library Association, 2011), 29–30.
9. Bourg, "Update on Our Library Facebook Page."

·········

CHAPTER 5

TWITTER AND TWO-NETWORK SUCCESS AND STRATEGIES

THE FIRST AND most obvious note about public library Twitter accounts is that there aren't nearly as many of them—and far fewer cases where a library has Twitter but no Facebook page.

Within the first 25 states surveyed (and libraries that responded to my survey), when originally checked only 35, a bit less than 1.5%, of the libraries had Twitter accounts but did not appear to have Facebook pages. Another 346 had both. When rechecked a few months later (using more extensive searching), while most of those 35 libraries showed only Twitter icons on the home pages, 19 of them *did* have Facebook pages with one or more updates, leaving a mere 16 Twitter-only libraries. For libraries in the broader 38-state survey, including those libraries, there were 896 libraries with both Facebook and Twitter presences—and only 57 that had Twitter accounts but no findable Facebook page.

This chapter offers a few notes on the 57 Twitter-only libraries, a broad view of the 953 libraries with findable Twitter accounts, and notes on how some libraries with both Facebook and Twitter use the combination.

It makes sense that Twitter would be less frequently used. A *lot* fewer people use Twitter. It's hard for libraries to announce events or provide details in 140 characters; in some ways, interaction with patrons works better on Facebook than on Twitter. And for libraries in less technologically advanced communities, Facebook will almost certainly have a following while Twitter may be unheard of.

· Exclusively Twitter ·

The libraries that use Twitter but apparently not Facebook are a varied lot. While there is none in the smallest library category, there are three serving 1,000 to 2,499 people (H1), four serving 2,500 to 4,999 (H2), six serving 5,000 to 9,999 (H3), 17 serving 10,000 to 24,999 (H4), 10 serving 25,000 to 49,999 (H5), four serving 50,000 to 99,999 (H6), seven serving 100,000 to 249,999 (H7), five serving 250,000 to 499,999, and one serving more than 500,000 people.

"Apparently not Facebook" needs to be qualified. I was unable to locate a general-purpose Facebook page for the library in my fall 2011 scan; however, five of the libraries had Facebook pages for children's services, teen services, or young adults, while three had Facebook links that didn't work—and one had a Facebook link that *did* work but went to a local judge's Facebook page.

One library had five tweets in a single day when checked, and eight more averaged a tweet a day (or five tweets per week). Eight had five tweets in a fortnight. What may be surprising are the number with less frequent tweets—five accounts with five tweets in a month, 13 with five in a quarter (and for four of those the most recent tweet was more than a month old), six with five tweets in half a year (and for three of those the most recent tweet was more than three months old), and a dozen accounts with so few recent tweets that they appeared abandoned: it takes *more* than six months (for 10 of them, more than a year) to go back five tweets. Finally, there are two outliers—a library with no tweets when checked and one with protected tweets: you can't sample them until you follow them, which is an odd situation for a public library.

When I looked at Twitter-only accounts in the first 25 states surveyed, I found none reaching even 1% of the community as followers. That's not the case for the more recent and larger survey. Eight of the libraries had followers numbering more than 1% of the potential patrons, including two with more than 5% (but none over 10%)—although four of those were occasional tweeters, needing more than a quarter for five tweets. All eight were small libraries.

As for actual followers, the count ranged from just over 3,000 in January 2012 (King County Library System in Washington, up from 2,965 when checked in early December 2011) down to two. Only one other library (Solano County Library in California) had more than 1,000 followers and none—when checked in fall 2011—had between 500 and 999, but 22, more than a third, had between 100 and 499 followers.

Since Twitter offers external observers more information than Facebook does, I can also tell you that the total tweets for these libraries—excluding the library that hadn't started tweeting yet—ranged from a high of more than 5,000 (Solano County) to a low of three, with eight libraries showing more than 1,000 tweets and more than half (29) showing fewer than 100.

Some library Twitter accounts followed the community of other tweeters closely, some did not. Five accounts followed twice as many as followed them, and another nine followed more than followed the library. Eleven more followed at least half as many as followed them, with 10 more following at least one account for every four that followed them. At the other extreme, four library Twitter accounts didn't follow anybody.

Finally, consider findability. For 19 of the 57, I didn't see an obvious link to Twitter on the home page (that includes King County, which also doesn't identify itself on the home page as being in Washington, although the Twitter account shows that information), but I found them via Google. That did include five accounts that appeared to be abandoned, which makes some sense. In seven more cases, I could find the Twitter account only in Twitter itself. The other 33 had clear Twitter links on their library home pages.

A FEW EXAMPLES

Here are details and sample tweets for a few libraries that feature Twitter accounts but no findable general-purpose Facebook pages. (As a side note, two of the three examples from the first draft of this chapter, based on the first 25 states, had to be removed because those libraries now have findable Facebook accounts as well. By the time you read this, it's quite possible that some libraries mentioned will also be two-network libraries.)

Anderson County Library

This South Carolina library serves 166,000 people from nine branches. Its Twitter account had 272 followers, followed 100 others, had some 521 tweets as of early January 2012, and averaged more than a tweet per day. The stream sometimes features items retweeted from other sources. It's used heavily to note library closings and events, as well as links to book reviews and items from elsewhere. Here are a few examples from two days in December 2011:

6in. to 4ft puppets in The Nutcracker by Becky's Box of Puppets for ages 5+. FREE! Main Library Tomorrow at 6:30 pm

---

Remembering Pearl Harbor [Link]

Homespun Holidays. Get some ideas and make an ornament. Dec. 13 at 7pm at the Main Library. For more information: [Link]

Gadsden Library

This Alabama library shows up as Gadsden Etowah County Public Library in the state library's spreadsheet but calls itself Gadsden Library or Gadsden Public Library on its home page and Twitter page. As of early January 2012, the library—which serves some 80,000 people—had 293 followers, followed 264, and had 1,387 tweets. The library tweets a lot, seemingly in weekly bursts of several tweets each. Four tweets from January 4, 2012, were all program related, but the stream also included retweets from others on a range of topics:

1/2 waCKy WedNeSdaY at 1:30pm and 3:30pm—come join the fun!

1/4 3:30 Wacky Wednesday today!

1/5 Kid's Papermaking @3:30pm. Learn how to MAKE paper!

1/5 STORY TIME AGAIN! The main library is open, so Story Time is back @ 10am

TABLE 5.1

Follows for library Twitter accounts

SIZE	POPULATION	FOLLOWERS	FOLLOW%
H0	2,602	179	6.88%
H1	43,368	917	2.11%
H2	168,833	2,498	1.48%
H3	626,663	8,635	1.38%
H4	3,671,763	30,448	0.83%
H5	6,356,732	26,008	0.41%
H6	10,503,411	35,040	0.33%
H7	21,841,887	57,915	0.27%
H8	21,804,207	39,139	0.18%
H9	59,900,252	98,025	0.16%
TOTAL	**124,919,718**	**298,804**	**0.24%**
Rural	4,513,229	42,677	0.95%
Urban	120,406,489	256,127	0.21%
Small	841,466	12,229	1.45%
Medium	20,531,906	91,496	0.45%
Large	103,546,346	195,079	0.19%

Solano County Public Library

This library system, with nine branches serving some 373,000 people in the San Francisco Bay Area, doesn't show its Twitter account on its home page, and it's a little tough to find via Google because the library leaves out "County" and "Public" in the account name. That said, it's a very active account, with 1,502 followers (and following 1,701) and 5,402 tweets in early January 2012, up from 5,077 in late November 2011. That's about eight tweets a day, seven days a week. These five tweets are all from January 4, 2012—part of eight that day, nearly all program related (note that FCC and JFK are both branch-name abbreviations):

> Want to do better in school? Join us for free Homework Help here at the FCC library! Every Wed from 4–6pm for kids K-6!

> Lawyers @ Your Library! Meet w/lawyers for free legal advice! Sign up @ 4pm & Consultations start @ 6! Don't miss out! Wed Jan 4 @JFK!

> PAWS for Reading! Kids ages 5–12 read to dogs & get a free book! Every Wed 3:30–4:30 @FCC library

> Celebrate Promises Made, Promises Kept: Tell us what you geek, get your Geek photo taken & meet Dulce the Clown! Wed Jan 4 3:30–4:30 @FCC

> Free Tutoring for Teens! For students 6th-12th grade! Wed 3:30–5 @JFK

Table 5.1 shows the followers for libraries with Twitter accounts as a percentage of the potential patrons for those libraries—and the overall numbers are pretty low. That's not terribly surprising, since Twitter just doesn't have the overall usage levels of Facebook.

Consider some of the other numbers Twitter offers to anybody who cares to look. Here as in most cases, these numbers include all 953 findable Twitter accounts in the 38 states, but not accounts for other libraries that provided comments.

FOLLOWING OTHERS

In all, library Twitter accounts followed 144,488 other Twitter accounts—just over 48%, or essentially half as many accounts as followed library accounts. That's an overall figure. For those libraries that did follow others, the average was about 80%—but the median was only 31%.

Fully one-tenth of the library Twitter accounts didn't follow any other accounts at all, and another 12% followed from one to five other accounts. At the other extreme, two libraries followed more than 4,700 other Twitter accounts, six more followed at least 2,000, and 20 more followed more than 1,000 but fewer than 2,000.

Percentages may be more meaningful here. Of the 857 tweeting libraries that followed other tweeters:

- Eight followed at least five times as many accounts as followed them—but there was only one library for which that was a substantial number, as the others had no more than 13 followers.
- Sixty-five other libraries followed more than twice as many accounts as followed them, and those weren't all libraries with tiny numbers of followers.
- Another 133 followed more Twitter accounts than followed them, with an additional 10 having identical numbers. In total, 206 libraries, or around 21% of all tweeting libraries, followed the advice I've read that a library should follow everybody who follows it.
- Eighty-three more came fairly close, following at least three-quarters as many accounts as followed them.
- Another 125 followed more than half as many but less than three-quarters as many (no library had exactly 1:2 figures).
- Fully 142 libraries followed between one-quarter and one-half as many accounts as followed them.
- Finally, 295 libraries followed some other accounts, but less than one-quarter as many as followed them.

HOW MANY TWEETS?

In all, these libraries tweeted just over half a million times up to the days on which they were sampled. That's a meaningless figure without context but might be meaningful for a future revisit. (See chapter 8 for notes on four months of change from August to December 2011 in 25 states.)

For what it's worth, the average was 574 tweets; the median, 259. Enoch Pratt Free Library in Baltimore, Maryland, had by far the most tweets with almost 13,000 as of early January 2012, but there were five other libraries with more than 5,000 tweets, 36 more with at least 2,500 tweets, and another 101 with at least 1,000 tweets.

FOLLOWERS AND LIKES

Although the discussion of two-platform strategies comes later in this chapter, it's worth noting one ratio: followers to likes. For the libraries with both Facebook likes and Twitter followers, the overall percentage was 48% as many followers as likes. The average of all these percentages was 81%—that is, eight followers for every 10 likes—and the median was 31%.

At the extremes, 68 libraries seemed to have much more success with Twitter than Facebook, with at least twice as many followers as likes (in six cases, more than *10 times* as many followers). Another 57 had at least 12 followers for every 10 likes. Sixty-four were roughly equal, with anywhere from 80 to 120% as many followers as likes.

The rest had considerably more likes than followers, and more than one-third of libraries on both networks—330 of them—had at least five times as many likes as followers.

Interaction is harder to spot on Twitter accounts, but some 260 of them had retweets or "@" responses within the first 15 or 20 tweets.

TABLE 5.2

Twitter accounts by reach/frequency code

	a	b	c	d	e	TOTAL
1	51	49	72	69	63	304
2	14	26	25	47	63	175
3	11	16	44	46	68	185
4	10	13	12	33	53	121
5	2	4	7	13	26	52
6	3	4	11	18	70	106
TOTAL	91	112	171	226	343	943

Table 5.2 shows the library Twitter accounts for which I could readily assign reach/frequency codes and the number of libraries for each code. For example, 304 libraries tweeted

once a day or so, with 51 of those libraries having very broad reach—noting that "very broad" means just half as much as for Facebook. That 51 is an interesting number, since the equivalent Facebook number is 55, although there are more than three times as many Facebook-using libraries.

As with Facebook, roughly 11% of Twitter accounts appear to be moribund (or are in a few cases too new to measure). If the upper left sector—at least fairly wide reach (a–c) and reasonable activity (1–3) is where most libraries would like to be, it's encouraging to see that roughly one-third (32.7%) are already there. Notably, that's very nearly the same figure as for Facebook. The other 56% of tweeting libraries have plenty of room for growth.

SOME EXAMPLES FROM THE TOP LEFT SECTOR

A total of 140 libraries are in the prime two-by-two square, with frequent tweets and broad reach. A few examples follow.

The Lyme Public Library

This Connecticut library serves 2,000 people. Its Twitter account has 370 followers (18%). It's the primary social networking outlet for Lyme, with six times as many followers as the Facebook page has likes. The library follows just over half as many people as follow it, averages at least daily tweets, and had more than 2,300 tweets in early January 2012. The active Twitter account and much less active Facebook page appear to be used for substantially different messages, as these examples—from two days in January—may show. If the length doesn't make it obvious, the first five are tweets and the last three Facebook updates:

We Bought a Zoo by Benjamin Mee. #fridayreads

Novelist E.L. Doctorow born 1/6/1931. [Link]

Actress Diane Keaton born 1/5/1946. Her new memoir is Then Again. [Link]

Umberto Eco born 1/5/1932. Latest novel is The Prague Cemetery. [Link]

"Once a president gets to the White House, the only audience that is left that really matters is history."-Doris Kearns Goodwin b. 1/4/43.

The side entrance of the library is open again. Lock fixed!

There is a thief in the library who keeps stealing my chair whenever I get up from my desk. The culprit is small, four-legged, brown, furry with a bushy tail and long whiskers. Must play musical chairs to keep her happy. **4 people like this.**

> **Lisa** Emma!

The lock on the side entrance door of the library is broken and stuck in the locked position. Please use the front entrance if you can, or knock and we will open the door for you. We hope to have it fixed within a day or two and apologize for the inconvenience.

> **Carol** Is this Prairie Home Companion?

> **Jennifer** Seriously. Miss y'all. Great library here but it is quite a different experience!

> **Lyme Public Library** Thanks, Jen. We miss you, too! Hope it's warmer where you are today. It's freezing here!

Princeton Public Library

This New Jersey library serves 30,000 people from a single location and has both Facebook and Twitter accounts, both noted in small but clear links at the bottom of the home page. When checked in December 2011, the Facebook page had more than 2,150 likes (7.1%) and roughly one update every other day, and the Twitter account had more than 2,300 followers (7.6%) and similar activity. Comparing five tweets and updates from the same period at the beginning of August 2011, there was no overlap between the two. While there was a little overlap when rechecked in December 2011, the content was mostly different, with the Twitter account richly interactive (heavy on retweets and @ responses). Both accounts show strong two-way community engagement. Following are tweets and updates from early August and late July 2011:

> Orpheus on stage during the reading of Eurydice @PrincetonPL ATT: @ brandonmonokian [Link]

> Eurydice on stage at @PrincetonPL directed by @brandonmonokian [Link]

> Our Page to Stage series is about to start with a production of Eurydice.

> The Monday Movie Mania series continues each week through the end of August, 7 P.M. start-times and free admission! Aug. 1—"The Adventures of Priscilla Queen of the Desert"—Aug. 8. "Willy Wonka and the Chocolate Factory" (older version w/ Gene Wilder)—Aug. 15—"Local Hero"—Aug. 22 "Mean Streets"—Aug. 29- "Pee Wee's Big Adventure." **[Wall] 2 people like this.**

"I just wanted to say that we really enjoyed the Seinfeld trivia event last night. We have a work colleague who is obsessed with Seinfeld, so we organized an after-work get-together around your event. The woman who organized the questions had clearly put a lot of time and effort into making it special, and her prizes and knowledge were astounding. We wanted to thank her for a great night."—*Laura* **6 people like this.**

> **Princeton Public Library** You're welcome. Laura. We'll pass your comments along to Susan Conlon, who organized the event.

> **Princeton Public Library** Da nada Laura! :^) *Susan*

A video quiz in anticipation of the 7 P.M. Seinfeld Trivia Night. (Items in the video will be given away as door prizes.) **[Link] Ellen likes this.**

Are any of these your picks for the best Seinfeld episodes? What else would you include? Top 10 Seinfeld episodes—Den of Geek **[Link]**

Hibbing Public Library

This Minnesota library serves 16,000 people and has Facebook and Twitter, both with clear icons in a "news" section of the home page. Here, Twitter is clearly the preferred network, with four times as many followers as likes. There's a lot of overlap among the items. The 604 followers as of early January 2012 (3.8%) got about two tweets per day. Here are a few tweets from two days in August when the library was having (and resolving) connectivity problems:

New DVDS: Arthur, Source Code, Sanctum, The Company Men, Madea's Big Happy Family and The Roommate. DVDs check out for 2 days. Free WIFI!

Our WIFI is back up and running! Thank you for your patience!

Split Second by Catherine Coulter: FBI Agents Lucy Carlyle and Cooper McKnight along with Agents Savich and Sher . . . **[Link]**

We a have a person working on our WIFI. Hope to be up and running shortly.

In case you missed it . . . : If you missed last week's deadline for the picking up your Summer Reading Program prize . . . **[Link]**

Checking the stream in January, it continues to be lively, with most (but not all) messages formatted to be complete without links.

Corvallis-Benton County Public Library

This Oregon library serves 86,000 people from four locations and a bookmobile. It has roughly equal numbers of likes and followers, with 1,051 followers and 1,168 likes in early January 2012 (in both cases around 1.2–1.3% of the community). Both networks see one or two updates on most days, and most tweets appear to be abbreviated versions of Facebook posts or retweets. Examples from early January 2012 include:

New blog post: This year I resolve to . . . [Link]

Birth to Six blog: Zero to Three Podcast Series: Little Kids, Big Questions [Link]

Check out the latest @CorvallisLibrary staff #reading picks! I added 4 new books to my "To Read" list! You? [Link] #read

---

RT @VisitCorvallis: Corvallis, Oregon News is out! [Link] ▸ Nice, thanks@VisitCorvallis

---

New blog post: Happy New eReader Year! [Link]

LEVERAGING TWITTER

Andy Burkhardt posted "How Libraries Can Leverage Twitter" at *Information Tyrannosaur* on April 26, 2011. Although Burkhardt works for an academic library, his comments (after two years of library tweeting) may be useful for public libraries as well.

> I have been thinking a lot lately about how we use Twitter and our successes and shortcomings with it. Looking back on tweets, conversations, and interactions from the past year and a half, I noticed 7 ways that we are leveraging Twitter to improve our library, our services, and our relationships with users.[1]

These are his seven ways (each has a one-paragraph discussion in the original post): report library happenings; promote library resources/services; build community; engage our users; monitor library-related tweets; solicit feedback; and create greater awareness of the library. Following is the paragraph on creating greater awareness:

> Doing all the aforementioned things creates a greater awareness of the library and what it has to offer. Being active on social networking sites like Twitter makes

the library more visible. Not every post gets noticed. And some that you think go unnoticed are actually effective. With [one post] I mentioned before, no one tweeted back saying what a good post it was. It seemed like it may have fallen on deaf ears. But not long after a student came in, mentioned he saw the post, and checked out a book because of it.[2]

· Two-Network Situations ·

When libraries use both Twitter and Facebook, how do they compare? Is there a different strategy for each social network or are Facebook updates simply longer versions of tweets? Does the library seem to favor one network over the other?

I can offer some crude numbers and comments from libraries using both in the first 25 states surveyed. You've already seen how followers and likes compare for all 38 states. The items that follow are only for the first 25 states. I would be hesitant to draw sweeping conclusions, but I have noticed that five-item samples tend to be reasonably representative in most cases.

- Comparing five tweets and five updates from the same days, roughly one in five libraries shows no overlap between the two and roughly one in five shows total overlap (the Facebook updates are either identical to the tweets or longer versions of them). The remainder are somewhere in the middle and are relatively evenly split among a few overlaps, some overlaps, and mostly overlaps.
- Roughly one-sixth of the libraries have a lot more updates than tweets (at least twice as many), and roughly one-fifth have at least twice as many tweets as updates. The rest are somewhere in the middle, with roughly one-fifth having essentially the same frequency (as measured over the 20 most recent tweets and updates).

COMMENTS FROM TWO-NETWORK LIBRARIES

Gwendolyn Vos, technology coordinator and webmaster at the Sioux Center Public Library in Iowa, comments on that library's use of both networks and how it has changed program response (the library serves 8,500 people and had 98 likes and 156 followers as of mid-September 2011):

> We use Twitter & Facebook. Our Facebook statuses automatically repeat as Twitter updates, which all show up as a feed on our main website (links below). On Twitter, we're connected more with other libraries, Iowa organizations, and local businesses. On Facebook, we see more connection with our local patrons, some libraries, some local businesses.
>
> For the past few years, we have offered online registration for the summer reading program. Previously, we've gotten a handful of online registrations. This year, because of our Facebook presence, we had hundreds of online registrations in the first few days, and the events with limited registration filled up pretty quickly.

Vicki Hibbert, director of Clive Public Library in Iowa (serving some 15,000 people), offered the following comments on that library's use of both networks—use that's apparently succeeding, as the number of Twitter followers is growing fairly rapidly.

> We have one staff person designated to handle our social media for both FaceBook and Twitter and a second staff person is trained as back up.
>
> In addition to promoting library services and programs she also uses both to promote 'good reads,' new media and to promote other cultural and literary events in our area and/or on the World Wide Web.
>
> FB is used for generating discussions about literary or cultural topics pertaining to new materials at the library while of course Twitter posts are much briefer.
>
> In addition to these library-related uses we also use both FB and Twitter to post traffic alerts or street closings and similar PR generated by the City of Clive Community Development Dept. During flood watches we post bulletins from our Fire Department or County Emergency Management Office.
>
> In a recent staff time study we estimated that a staff member spends an average of 20 minutes per day on our FB and Twitter accounts combined.

Consider three tweets and three updates from mid-September 2011:

A couple of openings for Tales with Tails on Saturday **[Link]**

A fab Chagall book for talking canvas w/ older children **[Link]**

Never thought I would be cataloging a Muppets album in rock, "The Green Album" to be added soon

---

Need to add a little groove to your day? Check out the link to see what music has been added recently to our collection. What artist/album are you diggin' these days? **[Link]**

"Beneath A Marble Sky" author, Jon Shors, will be at AViD tonight @ 7PM at Hoyt Sherman Place. Free. AViD 2011 **[Link]**

What are you writing? If you are a writer, you may want to consider the Montezuma All-Iowa Writer's Conference being held this Saturday **[Link] Benae Roorda likes this.**

Finally, consider a much larger library dealing with a difficult set of conditions in these excerpted notes from Donna Robertson, content manager, Digital Library Web Team, at the Christchurch City Libraries, a network of 19 libraries serving more than 390,000 people in New Zealand:

You might be interested in our use of social networks. It is slightly unusual, as it has been influenced by major earthquakes in our area. Twitter became an essential tool in spreading information to our community. We disseminated official information from various channels, and worked closely with the Emergency Operations Centre (and had staff working there). So our experience is a mixture of our tagline "Sweet treats for the hungry mind" and times of essential communication. . . .

Our basic tenet is "Share interesting stuff." We enjoy engaging with our customers and have a keen interest in what is happening in our area—so we share our discoveries. Heritage photos have gained lots of attention. People love the local touch and interesting snippets of local history. We promote new content and resources and point to things people may not realise we have.

We use hootsuite so we can package content for Twitter and Facebook at the same entry point. This also allows us to share new content on the website automatically. *Our team tweets using our initials and faces, so people know who said what.*

We respond to queries online, and try to be clear in our communications. If we are promoting a particular theme, such as Maori language, we schedule tweets so that the theme will pop up in people's streams.

Twitter: We have learned with Twitter that it really helps to have a snappy and enticing tweet. The same thing said wittily, or as a call to action, will get a lot more responses.

Facebook: We allow users to post on our wall, and ask questions. We use Facebook to promote events, not just our own but ones our community might be interested in. Facebook is useful in sharing and promoting blog posts and other new content on our site. [Emphasis added]

· Other Libraries to Consider ·

Following are basic numbers for two-network libraries in each size category, along with some libraries you might want to check out. These are libraries I haven't previously mentioned that use both networks and fall into the upper left quadrant for Twitter reach and frequency.

H0: LIBRARIES SERVING FEWER THAN 1,000 PEOPLE

There are four very small libraries with both Facebook pages and Twitter accounts, so 80th and 20th percentiles are meaningless. Three of the four have more than 5% of potential patrons as followers; the average is 6% and the median is 7%. The single library in this group that has both broad reach and strong activity (in both networks) has already been mentioned: Langdon Library in New Hampshire.

H1: LIBRARIES SERVING 1,000 TO 2,499 PEOPLE

The average reach among these 20 libraries is 1.9%; the median is 0.8%. The 80th percentile is 2%, and the 20th percentile is 0.1%.

In addition to those already mentioned, Lied Pierce Public Library in Nebraska combines broad reach and frequent tweets. You'll find it at @piercelibrary on Twitter.

H2: LIBRARIES SERVING 2,500 TO 4,999 PEOPLE

The average reach among these 42 libraries is 1.3%, and the median is 0.8%. The 80th percentile is 2.4%, and the 20th percentile is 0.2%.

Libraries with broad reach and frequent tweets include Hildebrand Memorial Library in Wisconsin and Preston Public Library in Minnesota.

H3: LIBRARIES SERVING 5,000 TO 9,999 PEOPLE

The average reach among these 78 libraries is 1.4%, and the median is 0.4%. The 80th percentile is 1.7%, and the 20th percentile is 0.2%.

Libraries with broad reach and frequent tweets include Stowe Free Library in Vermont, Lavenia McCoy Public Library in Colorado, Orange Beach Public Library in Alabama, Sadie Pope Dowdell Public Library in New Jersey, and Kimball Library in New Hampshire.

H4: LIBRARIES SERVING 10,000 TO 24,999 PEOPLE

At this point, we move from small to medium-sized libraries and switch from percentages of potential patrons to actual number of followers as a measure of reach.

The average reach among these 202 libraries—the largest group of two-network libraries in the 38 states—is 145 followers; the median is 64. The 80th percentile is 191 followers; the 20th, 17.

Libraries not already mentioned that combine broad reach and frequent tweets include South Sioux City Public Library in Nebraska, Lee County Public Library in South Carolina, Washington County Cooperative Library Services in Oregon, Rocky River Public Library in Ohio, Portsmouth Public Library in New Hampshire, Duxbury Free Library in Massachusetts, Maplewood Library in New Jersey, Wilton Library in Connecticut, Brooks Memorial Library in Vermont, and Yorktown-Mount Pleasant Township Public Library in Indiana.

H5: LIBRARIES SERVING 25,000 TO 49,999 PEOPLE

There are 169 libraries in this group. The average (mean) reach is 135 followers, and the median is 74. The 80th percentile is 208 followers, and the 20th percentile is 25.

Libraries that combine broad reach and frequent tweets include Bristol Public Library in Virginia, Westport Public Library in Connecticut, Mount Laurel Library in New Jersey, Westlake Porter Public Library in Ohio, Dover Public Library in New Hampshire, Cheltenham Township Library System in Pennsylvania, and Chelmsford Public Library in Massachusetts.

H6: LIBRARIES SERVING 50,000 TO 99,999 PEOPLE

Among the 139 libraries in this group, the average reach is 240 followers, and the median is 125. The 80th percentile is 395 followers; the 20th percentile, 40.

Some libraries combining broad reach and frequent tweets include Boulder Public Library in Colorado, Abington Township Public Library in Pennsylvania, Washington-Centerville Public Library in Ohio, Clackamas County Library in Oregon, Missouri River Regional Library in Missouri, Cecil County Public Library in Maryland, Santa Fe Public Library in New Mexico, the Public Library of Brookline in Massachusetts, Hamden Public Library in Connecticut, Anderson Public Library in Indiana, Mountain View Public Library in California, the Nashua Public Library in New Hampshire, and Cranston Public Library in Rhode Island,

H7: LIBRARIES SERVING 100,000 TO 249,999 PEOPLE

There are 126 libraries in this size group that have both Facebook pages and Twitter accounts. The average reach is 450 followers; the median, 233. The 80th percentile is 639 followers, and the 20th percentile is 67.

Libraries not already mentioned that combine broad reach and frequent tweets include Birmingham Public Library in Alabama, Manchester City Library in New Hampshire, Providence Public Library in Rhode Island, Eugene Public Library in Oregon, Arlington Public Library in Virginia, Springfield-Greene County Library District in Missouri, St. Joseph County Public Library in Indiana, Randolph County Public Library in North Carolina, Kenton County Public Library in Kentucky, Tacoma Public Library in Washington, Frederick County Public Library in Maryland, Abilene Public Library in Texas, Saint Paul Public Library in Minnesota, Worcester Public Library in Massachusetts, and Poudre River Public Library District in Colorado.

H8: LIBRARIES SERVING 250,000 TO 499,999 PEOPLE

Fifty-six of these libraries have both Facebook and Twitter accounts. Among them, the average reach is 661 followers, and the median is 382. The 80th percentile is 1,158 followers; the 20th percentile, 113.

Libraries with broad reach and frequent tweets include Virginia Beach Public Library in Virginia, Cleveland Public Library in Ohio, Douglas County Libraries in Colorado, Anchorage Public Library in Alaska, Howard County Library in Maryland, Arlington Public Library in Texas, Omaha Public Library in Nebraska, Lexington Public Library in Kentucky, Madison Public Library in Wisconsin, Carnegie Library of Pittsburgh in Pennsylvania, and Huntsville-Madison County Public Library in Alabama.

H9: LIBRARIES SERVING 500,000 OR MORE PEOPLE

Sixty of these largest public libraries and library systems are on both social networks. Among them, the average reach is 1,484 followers, and the median is 1,214. The 80th percentile is 2,428 followers, and the 20th percentile is 299.

Libraries with broad reach and frequent tweets (that haven't already been mentioned) include the Public Library of Cincinnati and Hamilton County in Ohio, the Free Library of Philadelphia in Pennsylvania, Boston Public Library in Massachusetts, Austin Public Library in Texas, Denver Public Library in Colorado, Charlotte Mecklenburg Library in North Carolina, Phoenix Public Library in Arizona, Orange County Library System in Florida, Tulsa City-County Library in Oklahoma, Pima County Public Library in Arizona, Milwaukee Public Library in Wisconsin, St. Louis County Library in Missouri, San Francisco Public Library in California, Montgomery County Public Libraries in Maryland, and Cobb County Public Library System in Georgia.

I won't claim that all the libraries mentioned in these size groups are the best examples of social networking, but I will claim that all of them are successful and may be worth a virtual visit.

NOTES

1. Andy Burkhardt, "How Libraries Can Leverage Twitter," *Information Tyrannosaur,* April 26, 2011, http://andyburkhardt.com/2011/04/26/how-libraries-can-leverage-twitter.

2. Ibid.

CHAPTER 6

FINDING THE LIBRARIES AND OTHER ISSUES OF THE SURVEY

THIS CHAPTER LOOKS at a few special issues for library social networking, including whether the social network accounts need to be linked from the library's home page, what to do about monitoring and spam, and what to do when it's clearly not working.

· Do You Need Links on the Home Page? ·

Most public library Facebook pages and Twitter accounts have links to them on the library home pages—but quite a few don't. Within the 38 states surveyed, I located 40% of the library Facebook pages and 16% of the library Twitter accounts through Google or the network itself, not by an obvious link on the library's home page.

As a library patron, and thinking as one who might be moving from one city to another, I believe I would expect to see Facebook or Twitter accounts show up on a library's home page, probably as the familiar F and T (or bluebird) icons. Having a widget on the home page that shows Facebook or Twitter updates isn't quite the same thing, in part because, for Facebook at least, that widget only seems to work if patrons have agreed to let Facebook do things some of us don't want Facebook to do. Libraries that don't want to serve as advertising sources for these social networks—and given Facebook's privacy practices I can understand that reluctance—can either use tiny icons at the bottom of the home page (as quite a few do) or have text links.

THE CASE AGAINST LINKS

I'm not ready to say libraries must have obvious links to Facebook or Twitter on their home pages. I checked the website of David Lee King's library, Topeka and Shawnee County Library in Kansas, since King is one of the best-known and most articulate proponents of library activity in social networks.

Guess what I found? The familiar F and T icons weren't on the home page when I checked in October 2011. But the library definitely had such accounts and had widgets showing Twitter and Facebook updates. Searching directly in Facebook, the library's page had 3,371 likes as of October 10, 2011 (about 2% of the library's service population) and a steady stream of interesting updates with quite a bit of patron engagement. There was also a Twitter account, @topekalibrary, with 2,099 followers (following 318 people) and 1,401 tweets, again with a solid stream of updates.

I asked King about this situation and received a convincing response, quoted here in part with his permission (from a September 30, 2011 e-mail):

> We decided to *not* use those icons pointing to social media for the present because our new site (up since March) is so visual, we thought they might get lost in the visual shuffle. And we have incorporated social media all over the place on the site. So Youtube videos are embedded in the appropriate places, Facebook, Twitter, and G+ like/share buttons are on every article, etc. . . .
>
> We decided something slightly different for now—that people browsing over to our website probably aren't our target users for Facebook or Twitter. It's enough that they can see we have them (and if so, they'll know how to find our pages in those services). Otherwise, we're really focusing on, say, our Twitter customers . . . *in* Twitter. Not so much on our main website page.
>
> Same thing with Facebook—we've built most of our Facebook tools for people already actively using Facebook (i.e., the Like buttons, the Facebook widget at the bottom of the page, etc.).
>
> And, most important, we share that we have this stuff. *Not* so much on the main page of our website—instead, we share it on TV (we have a weekly afternoon spot on the local news), we share it at the beginning of events and programs, in our enewsletter and in our print newsletter.
>
> As you say—active sharing in our community, and actively participating in those networks, seems to be paying off for us.
>
> I think you're correct—there isn't a single "do this" for social networks. You really have to look at your local community "audience," see where they're at and what they like to do, then create social media strategies based on that.

That final paragraph requires context—namely, the final paragraph in my e-mail asking King for comments, after I noted that, when compared to the libraries in Topeka's size range within the 25 originally surveyed states (214 of them, of which 141 appear to be on Facebook or Twitter), Topeka would have the third highest likes per thousand population and the second highest followers per thousand:

> At this point, I'm thoroughly convinced that there's no single set of advice for FB/Twitter use that suits every public library (and most public libraries still don't use either). Still, most of what I've seen so far suggests that the Facebook F and the Twitter T on the library's home page are fairly fundamental—but you're not using them, and you're pretty clearly succeeding. Comments, either for publication or as background?

I now believe that for every apparent rule or guideline for library activity on social networks there's at least one valid exception and possibly several. On the other hand, it may be worth noting that when checked in early 2012, Topeka *did* have icons and buttons for Facebook and Twitter. In quite a few other cases, icons appear to be missing from library pages because those pages are segments of larger citywide websites that appear not to be under full control of the libraries (or the city has Facebook or Twitter accounts and doesn't allow confusion by adding library-specific icons).

I'm still inclined to believe that for *most* libraries, and especially smaller libraries, it makes sense to have clear Facebook and Twitter links on the library's home page. Is there a way to demonstrate the worth of such links? Let's take a look.

· Distribution of Unlinked Facebook Pages ·

Here's how the unlinked Facebook pages break down by general size category:

- Among the smallest libraries, 82% lack obvious links. For the next smallest, the figure is 65%. It's 57% for libraries serving 2,500 to 4,999 people and 50% for those serving 5,000 to 9,999 people.
- Among the three medium-sized groups, less than half but more than a fifth of libraries with Facebook pages lack obvious home page links: 39% of libraries serving 10,000 to 24,999 people, 29% of libraries serving 25,000 to 49,999 people, and 24% of libraries serving 50,000 to 99,999 people.
- Relatively few of the large libraries with Facebook pages lack obvious links: 17% of libraries serving 100,000 to 249,999, 12% of libraries serving 250,000 to 499,999, and 11% of libraries serving half a million or more.

This suggests that, in many cases, links may be missing because the library doesn't have the in-house expertise to add them—and in some cases, the library doesn't control its own website (usually because it's part of a municipal website) and may not be in a position to add links. I'm inclined to suspect that most of the 17 libraries serving 250,000 or more people that lack obvious links have deliberately chosen to avoid the links, but that's certainly not obvious.

REACH, FREQUENCY, AND LINKS

I believe easy access to Facebook and Twitter presence through home page links will increase the reach of these social networking tools.

Table 6.1 shows the percentage of each category of Facebook page for which reach/frequency codes could be assigned, as discussed in chapter 4 and shown in table 4.2, that lack obvious links from library home pages. (As with table 4.2, some libraries are omitted because it's not possible to assign reach/frequency codes, most commonly because there haven't been five posts yet or because there are no likes.)

I find the case reasonably compelling here. At one extreme, 78% of pages that appear to be moribund don't have obvious links—and here I'm ready to believe that the causation is reversed: libraries remove links when they give up on Facebook pages. At the other extreme,

TABLE 6.1

Percentage of Facebook pages
without obvious home page links

	a	b	c	d	e	TOTAL
1	18%	13%	18%	24%	31%	20%
2	21%	20%	30%	29%	31%	28%
3	42%	37%	31%	35%	53%	38%
4	54%	39%	41%	46%	53%	47%
5	88%	81%	68%	59%	64%	65%
6	100%	71%	78%	68%	81%	78%
TOTAL	35%	28%	33%	38%	57%	40%

57% of pages with limited reach don't have obvious links—and it's hard to prove causation one way or the other.

Table 6.2 shows the equivalent percentages for Twitter accounts, as discussed in chapter 5 and displayed in table 5.2. Here I find it nearly impossible to make a case that reach suffers from lack of home page links, as the total row for reach seems to imply quite the opposite. I do believe there's a clear correlation between lack of tweets and lack of links—but, again, it's likely to be an opposite causation: if your library has stopped tweeting, it will reasonably remove a link to Twitter. (In some ways, 40% seems low for row 6.)

NOT PROVABLE BUT PROBABLE

I can't prove that providing live icons or links to your Facebook and Twitter accounts on your library's home page will yield more community engagement (which, in turn, seems likely to encourage more frequent and more effective tweets and updates). I certainly can't prove it for Twitter, as the numbers don't add up.

Still, it seems both probable and reasonable. More to the point is the reverse question: Why *don't* you have links to your social networks? I can think of five reasons (you may have others):

1. The library has abandoned the page or account and has chosen not to delete it. You don't want to call unwanted publicity to an account that's inactive. I believe this is the situation for at least one-fifth of the Facebook cases and more than a quarter of the Twitter cases.
2. You don't know how or are unable to add such links—either because your website isn't under your library's control or because your library lacks staff resources or knowledge. For libraries serving a few hundred people and some of those serving a few thousand, that's understandable.

TABLE 6.2

Percentage of Twitter accounts
without obvious home page links

	a	b	c	d	e	TOTAL
1	25%	16%	8%	9%	11%	13%
2	0%	12%	20%	6%	8%	9%
3	45%	25%	9%	11%	10%	14%
4	0%	31%	33%	15%	15%	17%
5	50%	50%	29%	15%	12%	19%
6	67%	25%	82%	61%	27%	40%
TOTAL	23%	20%	18%	14%	14%	16%

3. You don't want to provide free advertising for commercial entities by having big, obvious F or T/bluebird icons. In that case, I'd suggest using very small icons at the top or bottom of the home page or using text links instead of icons.
4. Your social networks serve specific purposes that don't involve the larger library community, so you don't advertise them broadly. That's an entirely legitimate reason.
e. Your home page is strongly designed and adding icons or links would weaken the design. Here, I would wonder—as I do about some strongly designed home pages—whether the design is getting in the way of functionality. Should your home page be a stunning billboard or a functional page for your community? I'm not in the business of criticizing websites, but as a library user, I know my own answer.

Maybe there's a sixth reason: Nobody ever got around to it. In that case, and maybe in some of the other cases, your library should consider whether obvious links are part of a strong social networking effort.

· Visibility ·

An obvious link on your library's home page is one good way to make your Facebook or Twitter account visible—but you should also see whether it's visible on its own. In other words:

- If one of your patrons looks up your library on Google or Bing, are they likely to find the social network accounts? For that matter, are they likely to find your home page?
- What happens if they look you up on Facebook or Twitter directly? Any luck?

As with some other issues, what I'm suggesting here is a "work like a patron hour" in which you seek out your own stuff as though you were a patron.

There's a secondary issue that affects Google visibility: Community Pages and other pages you didn't create. In many cases, even if your library has a Facebook page, the Community Page will show up first.

When I was doing the research for this book, if I didn't find Facebook or Twitter links within a library's home page (or didn't find a home page), I looked for Facebook and Twitter results (using the browser's Find function) within the first 100 results in Google, using the form of library name that appears in state library spreadsheets, with the state name appended. (In some cases, I expanded certain abbreviations and—if the library had a home page—changed the form of name to the one the library seemed to use.)

Most patrons won't go that far. If it's not in the top 10 or 20 results, it might as well not be there at all. And my luck with in-network searching has generally been rotten, especially for Twitter (where many library accounts use cute abbreviated names).

· Engagement and Spam ·

If your library maintains a Facebook page or a Twitter account, someone must monitor it regularly—at least daily if you're posting infrequently, several times a day if you're posting daily.

You need to monitor the account for two reasons, the second more important than the first (and the first applicable primarily to Facebook pages):

- People and bots will spam your page. Your library needs to decide what constitutes spam, but much of it is obvious. Is a self-published author's blurb about her book spam or self-promotion? If it's a separate message and the author has some ties to your community, probably the latter. If it's a comment on an entirely unrelated message, probably the former. If the message is about earning big bucks at home (as many comments on moribund library Facebook pages are), that's spam and should be deleted immediately. Failing to remove spam makes your library look bad.
- Successful Facebook pages and Twitter accounts engage the community, which means there will be comments on some of your posts and, quite possibly, questions as separate tweets or messages. If you respond promptly to those questions and messages, you enhance community engagement and encourage others to participate. If you fail to respond, you send the opposite message: This is just a library publicity channel, no community engagement desired.

Amber Mussman, public information officer at Cedar Rapids Public Library in Iowa, has this to say about monitoring the social networks—noting that the library (serving some 126,000 people) has both Facebook (707 likes) and Twitter (629 followers) accounts as well as blogs:

> It does take a lot of time to monitor everything, but I find that if you commit to spending the first half-hour of each day (or some allotted amount of time) to social media and the blogs, then you can manage things well. Our patrons use both Twitter and Facebook to learn about events and to have conversations with us. It may

only be a small segment of our population, but it is a very active group and they share information. When we write about something that people find valuable they comment or pass it along for us.

As I was continuing the expanded survey of libraries and writing this chapter, I came across a prime example of why libraries need to monitor all posts on their Facebook walls. A patron posted a polite request for the library's e-mail address, noting that the contact form on the website wasn't working. That should have had a library response within a day (better yet, within an hour). It did not. More than a month later there still was no response. That's one patron who now knows that the library isn't listening.

SHOULD YOU ALWAYS RESPOND?

Kathy Dempsey posted "Should You Respond to Comments on Your Social Media Sites?" on November 9, 2011, at *The 'M' Word—Marketing Libraries.* In the post, she points to an infographic offering a decision tree on when and how a company should respond to comments on its site, "The Social Media Crisis Communications Decision Tree."

While Dempsey's post deals with a range of difficulties in library social networking, only the last section is directly relevant here:

> [E]ven libraries that have good sites and that do engage fans by asking questions, still seem to struggle with the question of how to respond to unfavorable posts. When someone writes about a bad experience they had, do you reply publicly? Do you make excuses? How honest should you be? Should you remove the unkind comment and hope nobody saw it? Even the savviest socialites can be unsure of these answers, or can be held back by bad policies.[1]

Dempsey counsels libraries to use the linked infographic and "tell them that it was created by the U.S. military . . . and by a company that specializes in social media." I don't think it's that simple, but the infographic may be a useful tool. In any case, it seems clear that libraries can directly benefit through responding to patron comments (including hostile ones) and also directly harm their community standing by failing to do so.

But not all comments are legitimate attempts at engagement. There are various forms of spam, some already noted, and there are trolls who are *not* part of a library's local community but relish the chance to beat up on libraries for failing to follow the troll's own ways. I believe it's legitimate for a library to remove those comments, even though the infographic seems to say otherwise.

· Oops—Errors and the Human Voice ·

If your library's social network is done with the informality and human voice or voices that it should have, you will make mistakes. You'll say an event is on Thursday, November 17, when November 17 is really a Wednesday. You'll misspell a word. You'll leave out a word.

If this never happens—if every word is always correct and all of your tweets and posts have that perfect corporate neutrality of so many organizational communications—you're probably not using social networks as effectively as you could be. You're probably sending messages through too many levels of approval and editing, turning them into nothing more than PR.

The nice thing about errors is that they can help to humanize the library *and* engage the community—if they're handled properly. If people are liking and following your stuff, some-one will probably catch your error and comment on it. At that point, a casual "Oops!" response is a wonderful thing. I've seen quite a few of these on library Facebook pages (mostly smaller libraries, but sometimes quite large libraries), and it's always refreshing.

Of course you don't set out to make mistakes. But the rapid informal process that yields the best tweets and posts is also the process most likely to yield the occasional typo. Don't sweat it too much (unless it's a mission-critical message—and how many of those do you have?). Take advantage of the response, if there is one.

· Giving Up on a Social Network ·

What if it's not working? By "not working" I mean either your library doesn't find that its Facebook page or Twitter account is worth maintaining or, without any conscious decision, it simply hasn't been maintained.

As to whether an account is worth maintaining, you need to decide your own metrics. Chapter 6 of Laura Solomon's book *Doing Social Media So It Matters* has some good sugges-tions, both for assessing your success or failure and for what to do if you do give up.

My own metrics for deciding might be something like the following, assuming that you've had the account for a year or more, it has good content, and it's been promoted through your library's other channels and on your home page:

- If the number of likes or followers is still under 1% (for small libraries), under 100 (for medium-sized libraries), or under 300 (for large libraries), *and*
- If you don't see any significant engagement on the account, such as no comments and individual-post likes on Facebook or no retweets or responses on Twitter, *and*
- If there's no evidence that the social network is yielding other benefits to the library (bringing more people in for programs and so on), *then*
- Maybe the network isn't working for you.

Note that the first three bullets are "and" statements. If your large library only has 50 likes but those 50 are engaged and more people seem to be showing up for programs, then it's reasonable to say your network presence is underperforming but not a failure.

My guess is that for most small and many medium-sized libraries social network failure comes as often because of personnel changes and simple inattention. The volunteer who's been posting to Facebook moves away, the part-time staff member assigned to Twitter gets a new job, or it just gets too busy for a while and people forget about the Facebook wall. In these cases, this advice may not be very useful: You may have forgotten that your library even has a social network presence, and it's probably not noted on your website.

One of the macro-Heisenberg phenomena of looking at social networks hit me after I'd finished the survey and was preparing the samples (at the end of this chapter) of final updates and tweets. To wit, even though it's highly unlikely that a library will start updating again after an absence of more than a year, *it can happen.* One small library had its final Facebook update on June 25, 2010, when I checked it in October 2011, and started adding new updates in very late November 2011. Thus, while I'll still call libraries with no updates in a year moribund, they're not always 100%, absolutely, for sure defunct.

PULLING THE PLUG

Let's say you really don't see the point in keeping your Facebook page or your Twitter account going, or you can't afford to do so. What now?

Solomon's advice on page 56 of *Doing Social Media So It Matters* is excellent. Previously, I might have said that I had not seen *any* library actually state on its Facebook wall or Twitter account that there wouldn't be more updates and links to an alternate channel. As it happens, never is too long a time. In addition to a couple of final posts that come very close to being formal closures, I've now seen one explicit statement 15 months after the final real update: "This page is no longer updated—for the new page, please look for the [library] with a picture of the sign—not the library itself. That page is updated often. Thanks!"

Still, it's a rarity for there to be an actual closing post. That's unfortunate—just as it's unfortunate that some Facebook pages have apparently disappeared entirely (leaving Google searches that go nowhere).

You should post a final message (or for Twitter, messages, since 140 characters may not do it), explaining why there won't be updates and pointing to another channel. If there's going to be a moratorium—if the account is going on extended hiatus—you should also note that explicitly.

You shouldn't close the account entirely.

And you should do one other thing for Facebook pages: Turn off comments and the ability of others to post to your wall. Don't do this until a week or two after posting your final message, but unless you intend to have someone monitoring the wall for spam, you should do it eventually.

HOW FACEBOOK PAGES AND TWITTER ACCOUNTS ACTUALLY END

I'm anonymizing the libraries in these cases, but these are all cases where the most recent update or tweet is at least a year old (at the time I checked). I believe you can make the case that a few dozen more Facebook pages and Twitter accounts—those where the most recent update or tweet is more than six months but less than a year old—are also defunct, but let's stick with the clearest cases.

Here are some of the final Facebook updates, modified to protect the departed. I include dates in some cases, and in all other cases the date was no later than mid-October 2010. While some of these are very small libraries, some are medium-sized and one is very large.

> LIBRARY FUNDRAISER—Spaghetti Dinner (spaghetti, hot bread, salad, cake, drink) at the Legion Hall, Friday, November 12, 2010, 5 pm to 7 pm. Free Will Donation. FYI—Money from this fundraiser will be used by the Library Board to purchase book, book supplies & office supplies.

> BOOK SALE AT THE LIBRARY A book sale is in progress. There are many fiction and non-fiction books available. Hardcovers are $1.

Paperbacks, VHS, and Cassettes or $.25. The oversize coffee table books are $5. The library is located at [address]. Hours are Tuesday through Friday 9:30 A.M. to 5:30 P.M. and Saturday 9 A.M. to Noon.

Fall is in the air. . . . You have until Saturday, October 30 to submit your Flash Fiction entry. Remember short story must have a harvest theme, with the setting in [city].

Monday NOVEMBER 1, 2010 Moonlight Madness is back. We will be having the REPTILES this year. Future updates to come!!!

SUPPORT [college] READING PROGRAM! Event: Barnes and Noble's Day to Support [college] Reading Program Date: Friday, March 19, 2010 Location: Shop at ANY Barnes and Noble Bookstore Action: Use the Code below with ANYTHING you buy on Mar.19th, 2010 [code]. (Online shopping is now included. You can shop online from March 19th to 23rd.)

The [library] depends on the community for its financial survival and the majority of its staffing needs.

The [library] now has dvd movies for check out.

[Library] created an event. Book Sale Friday, June 18, 2010 at 12:00pm North Walmart Parking Lot

---

[Library] added 10 new photos to the album Christmas Village 09.

I will not be able to update or reply on this site for a while. If anyone should need a response, they should give us a call or send us an email for now. Hopefully we will get this all worked out soon. [May 11, 2010]

We're going to be closed on December 24–25, and Dec. 31–Jan. 1st. Have a wonderful holiday season! [2009]

I have to admit that the . . . wiki is taking all of my time! Please visit it for more info about the library! **[September 2008. The wiki in question *is* being updated.]**

A Summer Evening Reading with Eve Rifkah

A City so Grand: The Rise of an American Metropolis, Boston 1850–1900.

Should the library loan out kindle's? **[April 2009]**

[Library] added 4 new photos to the album Building. **[February 2009, with more recent work-at-home spam]**

New Adult Series . . . Books can be placed on hold by calling [#] Virgin River Series by Robyn Carr 1. Virgin River 2. Shelter Mountain . . .

The [library] will soon transition to a new Facebook account for businesses and public organizations. We apologize for the inconvenience that this is going to create. Please search for our new page under "[library]" and become a fan today! Any questions, please call us at [#]. **[June 2010. No new page can be found.]**

One Book One [state] Discussion **[April 2010]**

[Library] added a new photo. **[April 2009]**

Summer Reading starts soon! **[March 2010]**

come see Exotic Animals with Daren Handy at [location] at 10:30am today as a part of the Summer Reading Program! And they will be stopping by the [library] later at 1:30 today as well!

Welcome to [library]! Located in scenic [location], we have over 18,000 books in all categories, free internet access as well as wi-fi, audios, videos, magazines, art exhibits, and special programs! We look forward to seeing you! [January 2010]

Library Open Saturday, July 31st, BUT! . . . Due to library system technical maintenance on this day, several services will not be available: internet, on-line access to library accounts, placing holds or requests. We can check-out materials to you, but we will have to write down each barcode number, so plan on a little longer checkout time!

If you like the [library] please say "LIKE."

Our library is a community treasure. Come visit us!

Law seminar presented by [law firm] on April 28, 2010 at 3:00. The topic is wills and estates.

Interested in genealogy? Check out the [state] Room. [Link]

Want to know what others are reading? Check out the online catalog and see the Hottest title, author, and subject.

Today @ 3:00pm, Magic Show with Brian Richards! Come visit the library today, and Make A Splash!

[Local] Book Club: The Necklace by Cheryl Jarvis [September 2009]

[Library] added a new photo. [June 2009]

Our "Learn & Play with Me Today" session was a huge hit with toddlers and their grown ups! Information about our Children's programs can be found at: [Link] [April 2010]

Did you know the library's card catalog is online? go to [Link] and you can search the card catalog to see if we have what you need! You can also access your account and renew items online! (Contact the library first to get your log-in information.)

Author and trend journalist Alix Strauss will appear at the [library] on Wednesday, October 13th at 7 P.M. to help us celebrate National Reading Group Month. You should come—it's going to be a very entertaining evening!

Hello, and welcome to the library's Facebook page. Tell your friends about us and encourage them to join the group and become a fan. **[August 2009]**

The programs planned for tomorrow FEBRUARY 10 have been rescheduled because of the impending snow. The Fabulously Frugal program will now be held on Thursday, February 25 @ 7:00 P.M. and storyteller Veona Thomas will be coming in on Thursday, February 18 @ 3:15 P.M. **[February 2010]**

Twilight "Scene It?" DVD Game Friday June 25th, @3:00 PM. Come to the Library and show off your Twilight trivia skills and share Twilight treats!

Summer Reading Program—Thursday, June 10, 17, 24 and July 8, 15, 22 . . . Pool Party July 23 . . . Come check it out!!!

Here are a few final tweets, also anonymized and from at least a year before I checked the Twitter stream:

At Community Day (9/26) we'll have info on genealogy and the elections. We will be selling library bags, but no book sale.

The [library and school] need volunteers to be Reading Rangers. Call the library at [#] to sign up. **[June 2010]**

Garden Club started in [city]: Dig-It Garden Club. Already 40 people involved. Next meeting is April 1 6:00 p.m. [church]. **[March 2010]**

"Buy the Book & Bake Sale," Sat., June 19, 9–1. **[June 2010]**

Our annual Halloween Party is this Saturday, October 30th from 10:30AM-2:00PM! Everyone is welcome and be sure to come in costume!!

New YA Books: Riot by Walter Dean Myers; Front and Center by Catherine Gilbert Murdock; Leviathan by Scott Westerfeld. **[December 2009]**

HEY, REMEMBER YOU CAN GET FREE TUTORING! At **[Link]** click on the live homework help.

Over 40,000 people came into the Library in FY09. An average of 774 people a week! And a 21% increase over FY08! Way to go, [city]!! **[July 2009]**

Water balloon volleyball for teens (ages 11–18) tomorrow (June 29) at 4 P.M. Drop by and join us for a game or 2!

Wanted: 12 dedicated writers to join us on April 13th to launch "The [city] Writers Group." **[April 2010]**

Mondays in October! Tim Burton Halloween Film Fest! 6–8!

[Branch]: Movie Night—Thurs., Oct. 22 at 6:30 P.M. Classic horror film (call for title) rated R, 16-up, show ID. Free **[October 2009]**

Happy New Year from all of us at the [library]! We have a winter craft out for the kids this week when you stop in . . . **[December 2009]**

[Library] on air! [Radio station] at 11am! Author J. Michael Squatrito will join us! Call in and say hello! **[March 2010]**

[Library] has read House Rules: A Novel by Jodi Picoult **[Link] [April 2010]**

The Library will be closed Nov. 14–18 to prepare for its new online catalog and system. We will re-open Nov. 19 at 10 am. **[November 2009]**

[Library] hosts writers reading unpublished works of poetry or prose last Wed. of month at 7 pm. [#] for info. **[August 2009]**

New blog post: The Accidental Activist: My 750 Mile March with Tibetan Peoples Uprising Movement **[Link] [February 2009]**

Teen Summer Reading Party Thu, July 23, 2:00pm–3:30pm **[July 2009]**

Diary of a Wimpy Kid book release party Friday, Nov. 12 from 6:30–9 pm! Trivia, cartooning, games & The Wimpy Kid movie! All fans welcome!

MONDAY MOVIE 3/29 @ 7 P.M.—Rolling Stones Shine a Light directed by Martin Scorsese. **[Link] [March 2010]**

[Library] will open only from 1:30–5:30 p.m on Thursday June 10, due to a staff-only event. Visit **[Link]** for more info.

One specialized library Twitter account did end with a formal closure, as the project it was related to came to an end. It may be worth noting that six of the libraries with tweets immediately above do have Twitter links on their home pages.

NOTE

1. Kathy Dempsey, "Should You Respond to Comments on Your Social Media Sites?" *The 'M' Word—Marketing Libraries*, November 9, 2011, http://themwordblog.blogspot.com/2011/11/should-you -respond-to-comments-on-your.html.

CHAPTER 7

....

STATE-BY-STATE SNAPSHOTS

JUST AS IT'S absurd to treat public libraries of all sizes as equivalent entities, it's probably absurd to regard public libraries in all states as equivalent. Each state has its own funding systems, its own pattern of library systems and regulation, and its own character as a state.

This chapter doesn't get into funding or politics. I offer basic statistics for each of the 38 states surveyed and notes on a sample library in each state. Some of these libraries may have been noted in lists within chapters 4 or 5 but haven't previously had tweets or posts cited. These libraries may be outstanding in some respect (I believe every public library is exceptional in some respect) or may simply have interesting tweets or updates. I feature smaller libraries in many cases because so many smaller libraries seem to do first-rate work on social networks, and because smaller libraries represent the greatest growth possibilities for public library use of social networks.

What's the best way to arrange states in a discussion such as this? One way would be in descending order by population, and since I'm a Californian that might seem natural. It's confounded a little by the fact that we're discussing the sum of library service area populations and for some states that's larger than the actual population due to double-counting. Instead, we'll consider states in alphabetical order.

Tables 7.1 through 7.38 all have the same row and column labels:

- **Size:** Small, Medium, or Large—that is, having legal service areas of under 10,000 (small), 10,000 to 99,999 (medium), or 100,000 and up (large)
- **Libs:** Total libraries in this size category
- **SN:** Libraries with social network accounts—that is, Twitter or Facebook accounts
- **SN%:** SN as a percentage of Libs
- **SN LSA:** Total population served by libraries in this size category that have social network accounts
- **SN LSA%:** Population served by libraries with social networks as a percentage of total population served by libraries in this category (not shown)

The last two rows provide another piece of information that's frequently significant in considering why some states have higher or lower percentages than you might expect: the average LSA for all libraries in the state and that figure as a percentage of the overall average for the 38 states (41,405). States with low average LSAs will, all else being equal, tend to have lower percentages of social network involvement because small libraries are less commonly involved and vice versa.

It's worth noting that the overall percentages for the 38 states as a whole are 55% for SN% and 79% for LSA%.

ALABAMA

TABLE 7.1

Alabama public libraries in social networks

SIZE	LIBS	SN	SN%	SN LSA	SN LSA%
Small	125	47	38%	250,580	49%
Medium	77	38	49%	1,256,516	52%
Large	7	6	86%	1,442,496	92%
TOTAL	209	91	44%	2,949,592	66%

Avg LSA	% of 38
21,512	52%

Alabama's percentages are a bit lower than the overall average, with very few libraries serving 1,000 to 2,499 people involved in social networks.

Florence-Lauderdale Public Library serves some 85,000 people in Alabama. The Facebook page had 1,076 likes (1.3%) as of October 2011; the Twitter account had 106 followers (0.1%) and followed 203 accounts. Both accounts are updated fairly frequently and show significant user engagement—especially the @-heavy Twitter feed. Following are a few updates and tweets from early January 2012:

> Bookmarks Coffee Shop is open and ready to serve you! Coffee, pastries, snacks, sandwiches, soups (today is bacon and corn chowder) . . . stop by and treat yourself today! **Pat likes this.**

> What are you doing to celebrate game day? Many of our staff members earned their library science degrees at Alabama, so there's a lot of red and houndstooth at FLPL today! **5 people like this.**

> **Robin** Roll Tide!

A great article about the upcoming Small Steps to Health and Wealth series at the library. Starts this Thursday at 11:30 am! **[Link] Pat likes this.**

@BookmarksCoffee is open! Stop by for a coffee, snack, or lunch today!

There's lots of red and houndstooth at FLPL today! What are you doing to celebrate game day?

@danielrhorton But I definitely like the idea of some sort of recommendation system. Maybe some existing online service/app could help?

@danielrhorton We currently don't keep record of checkouts for privacy reasons unless patrons request it so they can access their checkouts

May I note in passing that it's always good to see a library citing privacy as a reason they don't retain circulation records?

ALASKA

TABLE 7.2

Alaska public libraries in social networks

SIZE	LIBS	SN	SN%	SN LSA	SN LSA%
Small	82	24	29%	66,751	58%
Medium	6	2	33%	24,314	17%
Large	2	1	50%	291,826	64%
TOTAL	90	27	30%	382,891	54%

Avg LSA	% of 38
7,891	19%

Alaska, a huge state with relatively few people, has mostly small libraries, one reason the overall percentages are low even as a fair number of small libraries are acting as vital community centers through their social networks.

The Tri-Valley Community Library in Healy, Alaska (12 miles north of Denali National Park) is located in the public school and is a combined-use library that serves a community of some 1,000 people. Its Facebook account has 112 likes (11%), provides frequent updates, and engages the community, as these examples from two weeks in late July and early August 2011 suggest:

> Thank you Usibelli Foundation, Totem Inn, Denali Glacier Scoops, Denali Subway, Black Diamond Golf, Princess Riverrun Deli and Miner's Market, for your sponsorship of the 2011 Summer Reading Program!!! **Ticee likes this.**

> 100 children, 10 weeks, 2,892 hours read. Thanks to our numerous volunteers, parents and program leaders for another successful summer reading program!!! Likes? Dislikes? Give us feedback for next year! **4 people like this.**

> Amazing cake! Thanks Selena! **[Wall Photos] 2 people like this.**
>
>> **Tri-Valley Community Library** Thanks so much Selena! It was an awesome AND tasty! August 2 at 9:37pm

> Tri-Valley Community Library created an event. Summer Reading Program Grand Finale Tuesday, August 2, 2011 at 11:00am Tri-Valley Library

ARIZONA

TABLE 7.3

Arizona public libraries in social networks

SIZE	LIBS	SN	SN%	SN LSA	SN LSA%
Small	44	7	16%	41,586	26%
Medium	31	11	35%	476,870	49%
Large	13	11	85%	5,226,649	95%
TOTAL	88	29	33%	5,745,105	86%

Avg LSA	% of 38
75,577	183%

Arizona runs lower than average in terms of libraries with social networks, partly because there's so little participation from small libraries—but above average in percentage of population served, because 11 of the 13 large libraries are on social networks and those libraries serve such a high percentage of the population.

Sedona Public Library serves some 11,000 people and is on both Twitter (123 followers, 1%) and Facebook (273 likes, 2.4%), with somewhat different content on the two networks. Here are three Facebook updates from early August 2011:

> Kurt Vonnegut Memorial Library offers free copies of Slaughterhouse 5 to students of MO school where book banned **[Link] 3 people like this.**
>
> **Walker** Kurt's literature ranks among the best on earth!

> Experience the VERDE RIVER exhibit and a reading by Thomas Lowe Fleischner from his provocative and uplifting book "The Way of Natural History." In this eclectic anthology, more than twenty scientists, nature writers, poets and Zen practitioners, attest to how paying attention to nature can be a healing antidote to the hectic and harrying pace of our lives. Join us Friday Aug 5th at 5:30pm. **[Wall Photos]**

> Every Thursday morning from 10:30 am—11:00 SPL will present a Tiny Tales program for babies and toddlers. Older siblings are also welcomed to join in. On the first Thursday of each month, Aug-Nov, enjoy a musical program with Kelly. Drop in any Thursday for toddler fun!—

CALIFORNIA

TABLE 7.4

California public libraries in social networks

SIZE	LIBS	SN	SN%	SN LSA	SN LSA%
Small	8	4	50%	12,969	40%
Medium	96	61	64%	2,905,735	64%
Large	77	51	66%	25,227,845	74%
TOTAL	181	116	64%	28,146,549	73%

Avg LSA	% of 38
213,521	516%

California has relatively few library districts for a state with the largest population, and very few small libraries. Although Florida has more very large library systems (serving half a million people or more) than California, California's 16 very large libraries serve almost as many people as all of Florida's libraries—21.8 million as compared to Florida's total 22.9 million. The percentage of libraries with social networks is higher than the 38-state average, and the percentage served is a little lower.

Sacramento Public Library serves nearly 1.4 million people from 29 branches. As of late November 2011, its Twitter account had 1,391 followers (0.1%) getting a tweet every couple of days, while its Facebook page had 3,592 likes (0.3%) and slightly more activity. The Twitter account seems to be unusually interactive. A few July tweets follow:

> @SteshaSims Yes, there are waiting lists but @saclib is awesome for making the Nook available to its readers!

> **Julie** (My 5 Monkeys) Fab Places I get books [account names]

> @ernietsmom Thanks for your guess, but the correct answer is actually Southgate. :)

Selected Facebook updates during the same period, noting that updates are signed and that "Name That Branch" is an ongoing feature that engages some in the community:

J.K. Rowling has followed in the footsteps of the great J.R.R. Tolkien by creating her own innovative words. What's your favorite Harry Potter-ism and what does it mean? /Megan **2 people like this.**

> **Jenny** Thestrals: the invisible winged skeletal horse and if you can see it, you've witnessed death. Yikes!

> **Susi** Dementors—I know a few . . . :) **21 hours ago**

Has your baby prevented you from learning to dance like the stars? Not anymore! Come to our Baby Ballroom program at Central Library this Sunday at 1 P.M., you can learn to dance with your baby. **[Link] 2 people like this.**

It's time for Name That Branch! This photograph was taken at staff preview day shortly before this library branch opened in 1976. The branch is still at this location 35 years later, and the distinctive lighting remains. Any guesses? /Amanda G. **[Wall Photos] 9 people like this.**

> **Vicky** Years ago (in the dark ages) I used to substitute at Southgate. I wasn't sure, but it looked really familiar!

> **Gerardo** Southgate

COLORADO

TABLE 7.5

Colorado public libraries in social networks

SIZE	LIBS	SN	SN%	SN LSA	SN LSA%
Small	67	25	37%	114,408	47%
Medium	35	16	46%	569,231	55%
Large	12	12	100%	3,696,012	100%
TOTAL	**114**	**53**	**46%**	**4,379,651**	**88%**

Avg LSA	% of 38
43,568	105%

The percentage of libraries using social networks is slightly low but the percentage of patrons served by such libraries is high, which makes sense given that all of Colorado's large libraries are on social networks.

Nederland Community Library serves some 3,300 people. Its Facebook page has 147 likes (4.4%) and a strong book orientation. Here are four updates from one week in August 2011:

> Books into Movies. Opening today August 10th "The Help." In September the library will host a 'book vs movie' discussion group on "The Help" in The Community Room at NCL. Date to be confirmed.
> **Jenny likes this.**

> Interesting article "Young People Are Reading More Than You" The State of Publishing: Young People Are Reading More Than You. **[Link]**

> 10 books you really should have read in high school. How many have you read? **[Link]**

> Books into Movies —"Sarah's Key" [Elle s'appelait Sarah] August 5th at Century 29th Street Theater—limited release so don't miss it. Great review: **[Link]**

CONNECTICUT

TABLE 7.6

Connecticut public libraries in social networks

SIZE	LIBS	SN	SN%	SN LSA	SN LSA%
Small	68	41	60%	227,282	65%
Medium	91	71	78%	2,047,576	81%
Large	5	3	60%	379,770	62%
TOTAL	164	115	70%	2,654,628	76%

Avg LSA	% of 38
21,203	51%

Lacking any libraries serving more than a quarter million people, Connecticut still gets more than three-quarters coverage by libraries with social networks—just under the 38-state average. That includes seven out of 10 libraries, considerably more than average.

Danbury Public Library serves some 79,000 people from a single location. While its Facebook account had 642 likes (0.8%) in late December 2011, its Twitter account had 1,606 followers (2%), the highest in the state. The two tend to cover the same ground, with the tweets written to stand on their own as much as possible. Here are four tweets from August 2011:

> Studying for your GED? Need job help? Need to brush up on your math skills? Learning Express can help. Find it under the Research tab.

> Flow Circus juggling, magic and comedy act in the Story Corner on August 18th at 11:00am. Don't miss it!

> Puppet show tonight full. Must have ticket for admittance. Check website for upcoming events: danburylibrary.org—click the events tab.

> Rango film showing on Wednesday, August 10 at 4:00 for grades 6–12. Free!!

FLORIDA

TABLE 7.7

Florida public libraries in social networks

SIZE	LIBS	SN	SN%	SN LSA	SN LSA%
Small	22	7	32%	27,853	25%
Medium	82	38	46%	1,330,906	45%
Large	42	30	71%	15,790,381	79%
TOTAL	146	75	51%	17,149,140	75%

Avg LSA	% of 38
157,041	379%

Florida's numbers are close enough to the 38-state averages to consider the state "typical"—a little low on the percentage of libraries with social networks and the same amount low on percentage of people served. (California, Florida, and Texas drive overall percentages to a considerable extent.)

Sarasota County Libraries serve just under 390,000 people from eight branches. When checked in early December 2011, the Twitter account had 384 followers (0.1%) and the Facebook account had 1,632 likes (0.4%). Both are active, with substantially different content in some cases. Here are three tweets and updates (all from a two-day period) showing some of a wide range of items:

> Which were the most used library databases in July? Anything having to do with genealogy: **[Link]**

> August 6 is Wiggle Your Toes Day. Paint your toenails, wear your best sandals or knit your toes some socks. **[Link]**

> July's most sought after listens: audiobook—**[Link]**

> Here's this week's question: How can the library help if you've forgotten the birth date of a close relative, for argument's sake, let's say it's your mother? (Yes, it's possible to forget your mother's birthday. It happened to m . . . no, to a "friend" . . . but let's focus on the question.) **2 people like this.**

Born to Read, [Link], will be one of the 50 kid friendly organizations at the Ready, Set, Grow Family Fair on Sat., 8/6 @ the Westfield Mall, 10am-2pm [Link]. We'd love to see you there!

And the winner is: "Cheryl's mind turned like the vanes of a wind-powered turbine, chopping her sparrow-like thoughts into bloody pieces that fell onto a growing pile of forgotten memories." The shortest entry to win the Bulwer-Lytton prize for the worst opening sentence to a novel. Click for more bad (but funny) 2011 winners [Link]. **3 people like this.**

GEORGIA

TABLE 7.8

Georgia public libraries in social networks

SIZE	LIBS	SN	SN%	SN LSA	SN LSA%
Small	0	0	0	0	0
Medium	33	15	45%	790,219	49%
Large	28	21	75%	6,544,426	84%
TOTAL	**61**	**36**	**59%**	**7,334,645**	**78%**

Avg LSA	% of 38
154,857	374%

What's most obvious here is that Georgia doesn't have any small public libraries as independent bodies; otherwise, the percentages are fairly typical.

The Lee County Library System is one of Georgia's smaller systems, serving some 35,000 people from four locations. It uses both Twitter (132 followers as of mid-December 2011, 0.4%) and Facebook (562 likes, 1.6 %), with mostly identical messages on both services. A few examples from a two-day period on Facebook follow:

We're going back to school! Lee County Library can meet your school needs. Check out our books, databases, downloadable eBooks, and much more! **2 people like this.**

Save the Date: Tuesday, Oct. 25th 8:00 AM—1:00 PM Lee County School System Bus Tour For more info please call 903-2101 or **[Link] [Wall Photos] Libby likes this.**

Book Club is back from summer vacation! Don't miss our meeting tomorrow @ 7:00 PM Leesburg Library. We will be discussing 'At Home in Mitford' by Jan Karon.

Start saving money by learning to become a Super-Couponer! Tangela Clements will share the basics of couponing in this program. Thurs, Aug. 25 @ 6:00 PM Leesburg Library. For more info please call 759–2369.

IDAHO

TABLE 7.9

Idaho public libraries in social networks

SIZE	LIBS	SN	SN%	SN LSA	SN LSA%
Small	75	18	24%	71,233	33%
Medium	27	17	63%	610,642	71%
Large	2	2	100%	309,905	100%
TOTAL	104	37	36%	991,780	71%

Avg LSA	% of 38
13,344	32%

With primarily small libraries and no libraries serving more than 250,000 people, it's not surprising that Idaho's percentage of libraries on social networks is low. The percentage of people served by such libraries is a bit low.

Coeur d'Alene Public Library serves some 44,000 people and has both a Twitter account (169 followers, 0.4%) and a Facebook page (473 likes, 1%). Here are a few updates from early August 2011:

A historical storyteller offers a program focusing on one of the region's biggest disasters ever Friday, Aug. 12, 7 P.M., at the Coeur d'Alene Public Library, 702 E. Front Ave. Ben Kemper will perform an hour-long original story, focused around the horror and the heroism of the catastrophic Big Burn of 1910. Admission is free. **[Wall Photos]**

Coeur d'Alene Public Library added 11 new photos to the album World Festival Summer Reading Carnival. World Festival Summer Reading **2 people like this.**

Sarah We had so much fun. .thank you guys!!! July 29 at 2:10pm

---

A program on Leonardo da Vinci and the Italian Renaissance and another program on the Big Burn of 1910 are offered during August at the Coeur d'Alene Public Library. Here's a video update of library activities produced by Jeff Crowe for CDA-TV. **[Link] Coeur d'Alene Downtown Association likes this.**

INDIANA

TABLE 7.10

Indiana public libraries in social networks

SIZE	LIBS	SN	SN%	SN LSA	SN LSA%
Small	134	69	51%	342,222	62%
Medium	93	79	85%	2,591,867	89%
Large	10	10	100%	2,322,919	100%
TOTAL	237	158	67%	5,257,008	91%

Avg LSA	% of 38
24,488	59%

Indiana scores well above average for social network involvement on both metrics, with more than two-thirds of its libraries (serving more than nine out of 10 potential patrons) involved.

Anderson Public Library serves some 75,000 people from two locations. Its Facebook page had 858 likes (1.2%) in mid-October 2011, and its Twitter account had 415 followers (0.6%). Both social network accounts are fairly active. These Facebook updates from early January 2012 show some of the range; most tweets cover the same ground but appear to be reworded so as to provide basic information within the limits of tweeting:

Brush up your job searching skills! Join us for Network 101 on Monday, January 9th 10:00am in the Delaware Room.

Anderson Public Library will host the Third House Legislative Meeting Monday, January 9th • 8am • Chief Anderson Room Local legislators are invited to discuss issues being considered during the session of the Indiana General Assembly and answer written questions from the audience. This meeting is open to the public and refreshments will be served.

New DVDs include The Hangover Part II, Harry Potter, The Help and more! Enjoy! [Link]

KENTUCKY

TABLE 7.11

Kentucky public libraries in social networks

SIZE	LIBS	SN	SN%	SN LSA	SN LSA%
Small	17	11	65%	79,768	65%
Medium	95	68	72%	2,151,275	77%
Large	5	5	100%	1,404,113	100%
TOTAL	117	84	72%	3,635,156	84%

Avg LSA	% of 38
36,791	89%

Kentucky has above-average involvement, with nearly three-quarters of the libraries (serving five out of six potential patrons) on social networks.

Henry County Public Library in Eminence serves some 16,000 people and has both Twitter and Facebook accounts—with a couple of slight twists. When checked in mid-December 2011, the Facebook account had 155 likes (1%), while the Twitter account had 324 followers (2%). There was little or no overlap in messages, at least in August 2011. Three tweets and updates from the same period follow:

The latest additions to our collection: This Week's Top Choices [Link]

Brown Bag Book Club: You're invited . . . to join the Henry County Library's new book club! Bring a sack lunch and . . . [Link]

The newest titles at your library: This Week's Top Choices [Link]

Resume building class today at 10:30am!

Don't have plans for your weekend yet? Join us for Lego Club on Saturday from 1:00–2:30 pm. This month's theme will be Back to School and for added excitement we will be making Lego crayons in the shape of Lego blocks and mini figures for participants to take home. Lego Club is free and open to all ages. We supply the Legos. You supply the creativity. [Wall Photos]

Henry County Public Library added 2 new photos to the album More Summer Reading 2011.

> **Sandy** Great pics . . . our kids had a blast during the summer reading program. We appreciate everything you do for families who love to read . . . looking forward to next yr. Great job to the entire staff :)

In case it's not clear, "Resume building class" is a very short Facebook update, not a tweet.

LOUISIANA

TABLE 7.12

Louisiana public libraries in social networks

SIZE	LIBS	SN	SN%	SN LSA	SN LSA%
Small	7	2	29%	7,855	22%
Medium	47	24	51%	791,826	53%
Large	14	13	93%	2,864,687	96%
TOTAL	**68**	**39**	**57%**	**3,664,368**	**81%**

Avg LSA	% of 38
66,215	160%

Louisiana, where most public libraries are organized at the parish level (similar to counties in most other states), lacks both very small and very large libraries and scores just over average on both social network metrics.

Union Parish Library in Farmerville serves some 23,000 people and had 472 likes (2%) for its Facebook page as of early December 2011. Following are examples from two days in early August 2011 on this generally active wall:

> Have you ever wanted to eat a 125lb. watermelon??? Come to the library today between 3:00–5:00 and eat a prize winner donated to us by Brookshires! Thank you Brookshires!!! **[Wall Photos] 2 people like this.**

> Join us today at 3:00 for the end of Summer Reading 2011 "BOPPIN BALLOON BASH"! Awards, games, and yes—WATER BALLOONS!! (This is NOT your average library!) Wall Photos **Angie likes this.**

> We welcome the Webelos of Pack 16 Boy Scouts at the library tonight. They toured the library and learned about Internet Safety to earn their communications badge. **[Wall Photos] Meg Wilson likes this.**

> Teen GIRLS-ONLY are invited to a Slumber Party mystery night this Friday, August 12 beginning at 7:00 at the Union Parish Library. Bring your PJ's for a night of girls fun including a mystery drama, fashion show, make-overs, and movie showing! **[Wall Photos]**

MAINE

TABLE 7.13

Maine public libraries in social networks

SIZE	LIBS	SN	SN%	SN LSA	SN LSA%
Small	238	100	42%	411,360	54%
Medium	31	27	87%	532,560	89%
Large	0	0	0	0	0
TOTAL	269	127	47%	943,920	69%

Avg LSA	% of 38
5,062	12%

Given that most of Maine's libraries are small, the social network metrics are reasonable: a bit less than half of the libraries and more than two-thirds of the people.

Cherryfield Public Library serves 1,100 people. The Facebook page appears to *be* the library website, and with 243 likes (22% of the potential patrons) and daily updates, it intends to keep its small community informed on library happenings. These three messages during a week in January 2012 will give a sense of how this works:

Open from 2–6 today! Yes, we WILL be open, unless this storm turns the roads into ice rinks we will be open for business. Residents of Narraguagus Estates: Don't forget the first Computer Class to be held in the Upper-Community Room tomorrow morning at 10:00. :-)

Open from 2–6 today! Any titles checked out this week can be kept until the 31st as we will be closed from the 24–28th! Perfect for those who worry about returning items late . . . you'll get extra time! ;-)

Open from 2–6 today! Our first computer class for the residents of Narraguagus Estates will be held this Friday at 10:00 in the Upper-Community Room (Dining Room). These classes will be basic instruction based on what YOU want to learn! We are very pleased to be able to provide this service to our community. **3 people like this.**

Diane Hope someone shows up!

MARYLAND

TABLE 7.14

Maryland public libraries in social networks

SIZE	LIBS	SN	SN%	SN LSA	SN LSA%
Small	0	0	0	0	0
Medium	13	9	69%	572,275	79%
Large	11	9	82%	4,578,704	94%
TOTAL	24	18	75%	5,150,979	92%

Avg LSA	% of 38
233,989	565%

Maryland has a mere two dozen library agencies, averaging 234,000 possible patrons each (even higher than California), and has no small libraries (none serving fewer than 10,000 people). The social networking figures are very high: three-quarters of the libraries, 11 of every 12 potential patrons.

The Enoch Pratt Free Library serves more than 630,000 people in Baltimore at 22 branches. When checked in mid-December 2011, Pratt's Facebook page had 2,510 likes (0.4%), but its Twitter account had 4,162 followers (0.7%). While the Facebook page is active, there are many more tweets than there are updates, including live tweeting for some library events. Here are Facebook examples from two days in mid-August 2011:

> JUST IN! Final figures for Summer Reading 2011: 14,099 kids/teens registered and they read 161,550 books! Way to go!! Summer Reading 2011 @ Enoch Pratt Free [Link] 8 people like this.

> "Wax on, wax off." Oops not that Karate Kid but the new one! FREE film screening of 2010's 'The Karate Kid' tomorrow, Aug 16, 2pm, Southeast Anchor Library. The Karate Kid (2010)—[Link] Bruno Sammartino likes this.

> Here's a major tease! AMNESTY WEEK IS COMING TO THE PRATT! When? You'll have to follow our Facebook status updates. :) Library Cards and Accounts (main page)—[Link] 10 people like this.

Edward I hope that the announcement of the date is given to the general public the same time it is presented on Facebook. I would think that those patrons most in need of amnesty would be those too poor, or too busy working, to either own a computer or have time to participate much on Facebook.

These are tweets from a two-hour period in early January 2012 (on a day when I'd seen at least 20 tweets so far):

YOU CAN STILL MAKE IT! PBS News Hour anchor Jim Lehrer talks about his new book, Tension City, 7pm, Central Library [Link]

So you got that Nook/Kindle/iPad for Christmas and you still don't know how to use it. Well . . . we can help: [Link]

@bwboncampus Yep! We'll tweet the pic. So look out for it. :)

McDonald's UK Switches Out Happy Meal Toys For Books [Link]

@yejese If Ravens win @houstonlibrary Director will wear a Ravens jersey. If the Ravens lose @prattlibrary will wear a Texans jersey.

MASSACHUSETTS

Massachusetts public libraries in social networks

SIZE	LIBS	SN	SN%	SN LSA	SN LSA%
Small	191	97	51%	464,098	60%
Medium	174	136	78%	3,711,066	80%
Large	5	5	100%	1,196,345	100%
TOTAL	370	238	64%	5,371,509	81%

Avg LSA	% of 38
17,887	43%

Massachusetts scores high for both percentage of libraries (nearly two-thirds) on social networks and people served (four out of five).

The Cushman Library in Bernardston serves some 2,200 people. When checked in late October 2011, the Facebook account had 114 likes (5%). It was and is active for such a small library. A few updates from five days in January 2012—including "Cushman Library" in some cases (normally omitted as overhead) because the update is worded so as to make it part of the message.

> Don't forget to register for our Digital Readers Workshop! January 23rd . . . two sessions, 3–5 or 6:30–8:30 . . . limit 15 people per session . . . FREE! **[Link]**

> Cushman Library will be open from 2:00 to 6:00 today. We still have lots of withdrawn videos up for sale, both adult and juvie. Drop by and see if any of your faves are in the pile!

> Cushman Library will be open from 10:00 to 3:30 today. Parents, we have lots of withdrawn juvenile videos up for grabs . . . 50 cent a piece or 3/$1.00 . . . come see if your child's fave is in the pile! We hope you make a visit to the library part your weekend!

> Cushman Library is filming the last readers for our community cable show "Cushman Reads" . . . it's all very exciting! **John likes this.**

Cushman Library It's very sad that we have reached the end of this part of the process. We have so enjoyed having all of the readers coming in and sharing their voices. Now it's up to Chris to work his editing magic. The first episode should be up and running by the end of the month!

MINNESOTA

TABLE 7.16

Minnesota public libraries in social networks

SIZE	LIBS	SN	SN%	SN LSA	SN LSA%
Small	90	37	41%	125,550	42%
Medium	32	18	56%	473,580	53%
Large	19	12	63%	6,539,332	81%
TOTAL	141	67	48%	7,138,462	77%

Avg LSA	% of 38
65,407	158%

Minnesota has libraries of all sizes, but most of its libraries are small. While just under half the libraries are on social networks, those libraries serve more than three-quarters of the potential patrons—almost precisely the 38-state average.

Hennepin County Library is famed in the library field. It serves more than 1.1 million people from more than three dozen branches. When checked in early December 2011, the active Facebook page had 5,967 likes (0.5%), and there were 4,619 followers (0.4%) for its more active Twitter account. Here are two of Hennepin's highly interactive tweets and three Facebook updates, all from a couple of days in July and August 2011:

> Janet And when I say picked up some books, I mean borrowed from the Hennepin County Library, the best library system on earth.

> @franske @petewall we have Consumer Reports online 1991 to present via MasterFILE Premier: [Link]

> What to do on a rainy day? Check out a museum pass! [Link] 4 people like this.

What's the next best thing to a grand slam? Free tickets to a Twins game! Kindergarteners-grade 12 can enter a drawing to win four tickets to the Sept. 20 or 21 game. Enter online at KidLinks www.hclib.org/kids or TeenLinks: [Link]

There are several movie adaptations of books coming to the big screen. Sarah's Key and the Help coming soon . . . do you prefer to read the book before seeing the movie? Have you ever picked up a book after seeing the movie?

Diane Books first and they were great!

James Normally, movies are so different from the book that I don't like them nearly as much. I keep thinking in the back of my mind, "That's not in the book!"

MISSISSIPPI

TABLE 7.17

Mississippi public libraries in social networks

SIZE	LIBS	SN	SN%	SN LSA	SN LSA%
Small	4	1	25%	8,116	29%
Medium	39	21	54%	1,029,222	62%
Large	7	4	57%	886,298	70%
TOTAL	50	26	52%	1,923,636	65%

Avg LSA	% of 38
59,201	143%

Mississippi's percentage of libraries in social networks is just lower than average, but percentage of patrons served by those libraries is significantly lower than average. It's still two-thirds of the total.

The Library of Hattiesburg, Petal, and Forrest County serves 79,000 people from two locations. When checked in early December 2011, there were 762 likes (1%) for the fairly active Facebook page and 205 followers (0.3%) for the similarly active Twitter account. Some examples from January 2012 include the following (note the interaction in the final post):

Family Bibles Road Show Thursday January 12th The Library Meeting
Room 5:00 PM Family Bibles Consultations [Link]

Join us for a viewing of the film "KJB: The Book That Changed the
World" 1/5/12, 2:00 pm and 6:30 pm, Hattiesburg Public Library A part
of William Carey University's Manifold Greatness exhibit. . . .

Just two hours til our Downton Abbey event—hope to see you there! (6
pm on Wednesday January 4th)

Christy Can't wait!

Holiday Hours: The Library will close at 6 pm on Thursday, December
22nd and reopen at 8:00 am on Tuesday, December 27th.

Steve Are there any plans to add e-books to your lending library?

[Library] The Library is studying offering e-books as a service.
Somewhat surprisingly technology is not the issue; cost and availability
of titles are the two major sticking points. The cost of an e-book is
slightly higher than what we usually pay. . . . [More]

Steve Thank you for your response. I appreciate your explaining
the difficulties in providing e-books for your patrons. Our library is a
wonderful asset to our community. Happy New Year!

MISSOURI

TABLE 7.18

Missouri public libraries in social networks

SIZE	LIBS	SN	SN%	SN LSA	SN LSA%
Small	82	34	41%	154,922	45%
Medium	59	34	58%	1,178,855	69%
Large	9	8	89%	2,947,606	96%
TOTAL	150	76	51%	4,281,383	84%

Avg LSA	% of 38
34,164	83%

Missouri's libraries are fairly close to typical for the 38 states in all three metrics measured here.

The Carnegie Public Library of Albany serves just under 2,000 people and when checked in mid-December 2011 had 212 likes (11%) for its Facebook page, which shows strong activity for a very small library. Following are updates from one week in August 2011 (two posts excerpted):

> Sponsored by the Friends of the Library: An open house for new Albany Carnegie Public Library director Jenny Ellis will be held from 3 P.M. to 5 P.M. Aug. 17 at the library. **Sarah likes this.**

> JUST PUT ON SHELF: YOUNG ADULT FICTION-*Die for Me* by Amy Plum [and several others]

> JUST PUT ON SHELF: ADULT NONFICTION-*Genius of Place: the Life of Frederick Law Olmstead* by Justin Martin [and several others]

> We're going to be starting a book club soon. If you're interested please check out this list of book club kits. I'll announce the first meeting soon where we'll pick out the titles we want to read. **[Link] Robyn likes this.**

MONTANA

TABLE 7.19

Montana public libraries in social networks

SIZE	LIBS	SN	SN%	SN LSA	SN LSA%
Small	61	21	34%	98,855	44%
Medium	18	12	67%	477,214	86%
Large	1	1	100%	123,097	100%
TOTAL	80	34	43%	699,166	78%

Avg LSA	% of 38
11,254	27%

Given that most of Montana's libraries are small, it's not surprising that fewer than half of them are on social networks, but note that despite this the percentage of patrons served is almost precisely typical at nearly four out of five.

Missoula Public Library isn't quite the largest in the state, serving some 96,000 people from five locations, but it has the largest social networking presence on both Twitter and Facebook. When checked in mid-December 2011, the Twitter account had 705 followers (0.7%), and the Facebook page had 2,613 likes (2.7%). Missoula seems to respond to each new Twitter follow with a "thanks" back and has more interaction than most library Twitter accounts. Four Facebook updates from a three-day period in early August 2011 show the human, small-library tone of this almost-large library:

> Check this out—literally! GL 920 SMALL Perusing our Adult Graphic Novels collection one day, I found this book by David Small. Stitches, a Memoir is set during the years 1951–1990. . . .

> The latest creation from author, Alice Hoffman, due out October . . .
> **[Link] Anni likes this.**

> Today is the first day of the Western Montana Fair. What does that have to do with the library? Let us know if you figure it out once you've paid a visit to the fair.

> **Jillian** Is the bookmobile having a rendezvous with tater pigs?

Missoula Public Library Nice try Jillian. Let me know again once you've visited the fair.

Missoula Public Library We had lots of visitors yesterday. Stop by and say hi today if you're at the WMF.

Good news, everyone! This really is good news, not Professor Farnsworth-type good news. Futurama: The Complete Collection will be available for checkout soon. **5 people like this.**

NEBRASKA

TABLE 7.20

Nebraska public libraries in social networks

SIZE	LIBS	SN	SN%	SN LSA	SN LSA%
Small	253	80	32%	178,103	52%
Medium	14	13	93%	341,506	95%
Large	2	2	100%	780,263	100%
TOTAL	269	95	35%	1,299,872	88%

Avg LSA	% of 38
5,499	13%

Most of Nebraska's public libraries are very small, with more than 80% serving fewer than 2,500 people. Just over one-third of the libraries are on social networks, and the fact that 15 of 16 medium and large libraries are involved accounts for the higher-than-average percentage of patrons served by libraries with social networks.

Omaha Public Library is about as atypical a Nebraska library as you can get, serving nearly 499,000 people from a dozen locations and its service area population being more than one-third of Nebraska's total. When checked in late October 2011, its Facebook page had 3,380 likes (0.7%), and its Twitter account had 1,103 followers (0.2%). Both accounts have very frequent updates. The two accounts don't always have the same information, as these tweets and (signed) updates from one day in January 2012 suggest:

We had so much fun in #2011! Look back at @OmahaLibrary events and programs—OPL: A Year in Photos 2011 video **[Link]**

Like our events? Tell your Facebook friends! Find an event on our calendar and click "Like" at the top right to share. [Link]

2011 was a great year at OPL! Take a look back on some of the good times we shared. Do you have a favorite memory or program? /Emily Omaha Public Library—A Year in Photos 2011 [Link] 6 people like this.

> **Amy** LOVE this!

> **Pat** NICE!

We met a couple yesterday who met at our Speed Dating event last year and now describe their relationship as "serious." It's your turn now! Sign up today! /Emily [More] 6 people like this.

> **Omaha Public Library** Sometimes we meet people in the most unlikely ways. For those of you who are attached, how did you meet your significant other? /Emily

> **Amy** I met my beau at a gallery opening at Dixie Quick's. Couple months later, we met again at the Restore Omaha conference where I issued him an OPL library card. We started dating a few weeks later.

NEVADA

TABLE 7.21

Nevada public libraries in social networks

SIZE	LIBS	SN	SN%	SN LSA	SN LSA%
Small	10	2	20%	14,095	37%
Medium	8	5	63%	211,401	65%
Large	4	3	75%	2,160,204	91%
TOTAL	22	10	45%	2,385,700	87%

Avg LSA	% of 38
124,488	301%

Nevada has three libraries serving more than a quarter million people, all on social networks and collectively serving nearly four out of five Nevada residents. Thus, the percentage of patrons served by networking libraries is very high, even though less than half of the libraries are on social networks.

The Washoe County Library System serves some 424,000 people from a dozen locations in Reno, Sparks, and surrounding areas. While the system maintains both a Twitter account and a Facebook page, the Twitter account was only a few months old and not yet well used or frequently updated when checked in December 2011, with only a dozen followers and 28 tweets. At the time, its content was *entirely* separate from the Facebook page, which had the most likes of any Nevada public library with 1,041 (0.3%) and a varied, active stream of updates. Here are examples from a week in August 2011:

> Sierra View Library in Reno Town Mall is hosting a Science Fiction Film Fest on Tues., Aug. 16, to welcome Renovation, the 69th World Science Fiction Convention. Noon, "The Brain That Wouldn't Die;" 1:15 pm, "Santa Claus Conquers the Martians;" 2:45 pm, "Phantom Planet;" 4:15 pm, "Petrified World," 5:30 pm, "Crash of the Moons." This fantastic film fest will be followed by "Authors in the Library" at Sierra View on Wed., Aug. 17. **2 people like this.**

> Ringling Bros. and Barnum & Bailey Circus clowns will present special storytimes at four libraries! Meet the Ambassadors of Laughter: Mon., Aug. 22, 10:30 A.M., Spanish Springs; Tues. Aug. 23, 11:15 A.M., Sierra View and 4 P.M., Downtown Reno; and Wed., Aug. 24, 11:15 A.M., South

Valleys. Magic, reading and fun for everyone! **[Wall Photos] 3 people like this.**

Know someone interested in learning to navigate the information superhighway? Introduction to the Internet class today at Sparks Library, 1 pm. **2 people like this.**

Friends of Washoe County Library will hold a book sale Aug. 13 and 14 at 125 Gentry Way. Hours are 9-10 A.M. Saturday for Friends members and 10 A.M.-5 P.M. for the general public. Sunday hours are 10 A.M.-4 P.M. In addition, there will be a "library surplus" book sale on Saturday, Aug. 20, from 7 A.M.-2 P.M. at 5205 Mill St. Lots of good buys to be found at both sales! **[Link] 3 people like this.**

NEW HAMPSHIRE

TABLE 7.22

New Hampshire public libraries in social networks

SIZE	LIBS	SN	SN%	SN LSA	SN LSA%
Small	198	100	51%	375,804	57%
Medium	31	21	68%	493,961	72%
Large	1	1	100%	108,625	100%
TOTAL	230	122	53%	978,390	67%

Avg LSA	% of 38
6,308	15%

New Hampshire also has relatively few people, no very large libraries, and mostly small libraries. While a majority of libraries are on social networks, the percentage of patrons served by those libraries—while still two-thirds—is below average.

Effingham Public Library serves 1,500 people and had 165 likes (11%) for its Facebook page when checked in early November 2011. The page has variably frequent updates, such as these from late December 2011:

"Fiction reveals truth that reality obscures." ~ Jessamyn West **2 people like this.**

To all of our patrons and friends: have a happy, healthy and safe Holiday Season!

Kathy You too guys!

Effingham Public Library added 16 new photos to the album December 17, 2011. Effingham Public Library 2011 Christmas Party- Santa read THE POLAR EXPRESS by Chris van Allsburg, and handed out candy canes and presents for everyone! We all had a great time- especially Santa!

Maria I am glad everyone had a good time. We did not get to go because Arabella is not feeling well.

Effingham Public Library Sorry you couldn't make it. Hope she feels better soon!

Maria Thank you. She is starting to feel better already.

Santa will be stopping in for a visit with us at 12:30 today- come on in and share some holiday stories and enjoy some light refreshments!

Donna My daughter had a good time. Merry Christmas to you all and thanks for all you do!

Effingham Public Library Thank you, Donna. We have as much fun as the kids do . . . maybe even more!

NEW JERSEY

TABLE 7.23

New Jersey public libraries in social networks

SIZE	LIBS	SN	SN%	SN LSA	SN LSA%
Small	121	51	42%	340,757	47%
Medium	168	117	70%	3,411,172	71%
Large	14	13	93%	3,300,239	95%
TOTAL	303	181	60%	7,052,168	78%

Avg LSA	% of 38
29,800	72%

New Jersey scores slightly above average for public library involvement in social networks and almost precisely average for patrons served by networking libraries.

One of New Jersey's smallest libraries, Cranbury Public Library, serves some 3,200 people and maintains an active Twitter account (169 followers, 5.2%) and a very active Facebook account with 226 friends (7%) rather than likes, since it's a regular account under "Cran Bury" rather than a page. The two feeds aren't identical, although there's some overlap. Examples of Facebook updates from a two-day period in late July 2011 include:

> Open Gaming @ The Library Recurring Event First start: 2011–09–08 15:30:00 EDT . . .

> Cranbury Unveils Plans for New Library—East Windsor, [Link]

> New post: Tonight!! Libraryfest!!! July 27 at 7:00 P.M. Join us for Indian Dancing [Link]

> Arthritis Can Affect Anyone, When: Thu Oct 20, 2011 7pm to Thu Oct 20, 2011 8pm EDT

NEW MEXICO

TABLE 7.24

New Mexico public libraries in social networks

SIZE	LIBS	SN	SN%	SN LSA	SN LSA%
Small	69	20	29%	66,528	33%
Medium	19	9	47%	348,266	65%
Large	3	3	100%	846,491	100%
TOTAL	91	32	35%	1,261,285	79%

Avg LSA	% of 38
17,461	42%

New Mexico, with mostly small libraries but one very large library, is an odd case: while just over one-third of the libraries are on social networks, the percentage of potential patrons served by those libraries is precisely the 38-state average of 79%. That's because one library serves nearly 40% of the state, and the six largest libraries, all of which are on social networks, serve two-thirds of the state's population.

Questa Public Library serves a community of 1,900 people. Its Facebook page has 191 likes (10%). Following are four updates from the end of December 2011 and into January 2012:

> We are working on a description of how to register and use your new Kindle. It will be available on our website: www.questalibrary.org. Visit us soon and click on the blog site. **[Link]**

> **Questa Public Library** The blog has been published. Sharon is going to fine tune it and add some information tomorrow. We've also included sites that offer free ebooks.

> Look for our new ART section! It's located under the south windows on the adult side of the library. We have books about artists, their work, museum stories and exhibits. Most have come to us from an art grant that we receive every year. The remainder have been donated by generous patrons.

> We are open today, January 2, 12–4 PM. Start off the New Year with a visit to the library! Internet is working right now! **Denise W. likes this.**

> **Denise** yay!

Ice in the parking lot has been sanded. We have a small book sale going on now until the books are sold. .25 for paperbacks .50 for hard backs. .25 for CDs .50 for movies (VHS). We also have some young adult books for .25. HUGE savings. All to make room for new books! **Denise W. likes this.**

NORTH CAROLINA

TABLE 7.25

North Carolina public libraries in social networks

SIZE	LIBS	SN	SN%	SN LSA	SN LSA%
Small	2	1	50%	4,776	49%
Medium	43	27	63%	1,585,386	71%
Large	32	21	66%	5,418,062	76%
TOTAL	**77**	**49**	**64%**	**7,008,224**	**75%**

Avg LSA	% of 38
121,852	294%

North Carolina has almost no small libraries—none in the two smallest groups, one each in the next two. Nearly two-thirds of the libraries are on social networks, considerably more than average, and three-quarters of patrons (just under average) are served by those libraries.

The Transylvania County Library serves 31,000 people, 2.4% of them (753) liking its Facebook account when checked in mid-December 2011. That's the highest percentage of any North Carolina library. Examples include:

Strike up the Band! Don't miss "Winds of Change" the pictorial display on Transylvania County's Bands on the Second Floor **[Wall Photos] Share**

We heard you! Close to 1200 library users took our survey. THANK YOU for your compliments and suggestions! We will share the results with you soon. . . . **Jennifer likes this.**

Don't forget tonight! Looks like it'll be a beautiful night for an outdoor concert. Come check it out at 7:30 p.m. **[Link] Steven likes this.**

═══════ OHIO ═══════

TABLE 7.26

Ohio public libraries in social networks

SIZE	LIBS	SN	SN%	SN LSA	SN LSA%
Small	88	59	67%	357,227	71%
Medium	139	111	80%	3,734,495	83%
Large	24	21	88%	6,142,500	94%
TOTAL	251	191	76%	10,234,222	89%

Avg LSA	% of 38
45,984	111%

Although Ohio has a fairly typical variety of library sizes, it's not at all typical in two respects: three-quarters of the libraries are on social networks, and almost nine out of 10 potential patrons are served by those libraries.

Tipp City Public Library is far from being Ohio's largest (it serves some 14,800 people) and far from having the most Facebook likes (that's Columbus Metropolitan with 22,142, the highest in the 38 states but not the nation). However, it does participate in both networks and has very high reach: as of early November 2011, 1,988 likes (13.5%) and 750 Twitter followers (5.1%). Here are a few updates from early January 2012 (tweets are mostly shorter versions of the same items):

> National Arts and Humanities Youth Program Awards [Link] "These outstanding programs are expanding horizons, changing lives, and helping young people fulfill their dreams—across America and around the world. Each of these programs is using achievement in the arts and humanities as a bridge to achievement in life."

> Sips and Sneak Previews! Jan 13, 10:30–11:30am Stop by for coffee, donuts & book talks focusing on new releases just about to hit the shelves!

> Sock Knitting Group! Wed, January 11, 2pm–3pm Knitters: Isn't it time you learned how to knit socks? Join this weekly knitting group on Wednesdays to learn the basics of knitting in the round on five needles. The program leader will also have tips for new knitters. Please bring your own knitting needles.

OKLAHOMA

TABLE 7.27

Oklahoma public libraries in social networks

SIZE	LIBS	SN	SN%	SN LSA	SN LSA%
Small	0	0	0	0	0
Medium	3	2	67%	123,588	73%
Large	5	4	80%	1,838,934	88%
TOTAL	8	6	75%	1,962,522	87%

Avg LSA	% of 38
281,244	679%

Oklahoma has a uniquely small number of public library agencies with none small and more than half large. Both percentage of libraries on social networks and percentage of patrons served by those libraries are well above average.

The Metropolitan Library System in Oklahoma County serves some 716,000 people with 17 locations. Its Facebook account when checked in mid-December 2011 had 3,802 likes (0.5%), and its Twitter account had 2,193 followers (0.3%). The two accounts have substantially different content, and the Facebook wall shows personal voices that you might not expect from such a large institution, as in these mid-August 2011 updates:

> I've had 4 books come in from reserve Friday and today. How am I supposed to read them all?! Plus the 2 eBooks that came in. Shoulda taken that speed reading course in college. . . . **6 people like this.**
>
> **Emily** I know. I have three ebooks lined up to read. I had to reserve them because if I waited til I was ready then no telling how long a wait I would have. I usually get through a book in three days anyway.
>
> **Jan** i have that same problem all the time! **2 hours ago**

> Our after school art programs start in September at eight library locations around the metro! **[Wall Photos] 10 people like this.**

Working on September Library Card month stuff and missing Big Brother
. . . sniff sniff ::how's Rachel surviving without Brendan???::

> **Dana** she needs to girl up and realize she doesn't need her "man"
> to be a strong player.

> **Tracey** noone comes between me and my man . . . she is so
> insecure! its annoying!

Got a hankerin' to write a romance novel? Get some tips from author
Lacy Williams @ the Belle Isle Library, Tuesday August/16, 7–8:30pm.
Stop by the info desk or call 843-9601 to sign up! **3 people like this.**

Is a post about Big Brother appropriate for a library Facebook account that potentially
reaches almost three-quarters of a million people? If one goal is community engagement
and another is to make the library a human place, I find it hard to quarrel with what's happening here.

OREGON

TABLE 7.28

Oregon public libraries in social networks

SIZE	LIBS	SN	SN%	SN LSA	SN LSA%
Small	68	18	26%	74,824	32%
Medium	53	37	70%	1,218,796	78%
Large	8	7	88%	1,766,546	94%
TOTAL	129	62	48%	3,060,166	84%

Avg LSA	% of 38
28,363	69%

Fewer than half of Oregon's mostly small libraries are on social networks, but five out of
six people are served by libraries on a social network, which is a bit higher than the 38-state
average.

Lake Oswego Library serves some 37,000 people from a single location and has a healthy
social network presence, with 222 followers (0.6%) on Twitter and 696 likes (1.9%) on Facebook
as of mid-December 2011. When checked in mid-August, there was little or no overlap between
tweets and updates. Here are four updates over a three-day period:

Yikes, the college essay! College Advisor Tim Cantrick explains the essentials of a good application essay at a workshop on Tuesday, August 23 at 2:00 P.M. at Lake Oswego Library. Register at 503-697-6580. **[Wall Photos]**

Exciting news! Today we are announcing that Mink River by Lake Oswego's own Brian Doyle has been selected as the 2012 Lake Oswego Reads book. Programs based on the book will be in February, and the Friends of the LO Library will provide free books on January 9, 2012. Books are available now at the Library or at Graham's Book Store. Audio books and ebooks will be available soon. We can't wait for February! **[Link] 6 people like this.**

Today! The Umpqua Bank Ice Cream Truck will park outside the Library from 1 to 1:45 pm to distribute *free ice cream!* Watch the Knights of Veritas at noon just down the street at Rossman Park, then come up to the Library for a sweet treat. **7 people like this.**

Reminder: The Knights of Veritas will perform tomorrow at noon. They will introduce the Code of Chivalry to a modern audience and pit myth against fact with thrilling demonstrations of historical combat technique! This all-ages event will be held at Rossman Park, just down the street at 555 Fourth St (not at the library!). Performing Arts Series: Knights of Veritas Location: Rossman Park Time: 12:00PM Wednesday, August 17th **4 people like this.**

PENNSYLVANIA

TABLE 7.29

Pennsylvania public libraries in social networks

SIZE	LIBS	SN	SN%	SN LSA	SN LSA%
Small	188	95	51%	533,208	56%
Medium	252	192	76%	5,447,474	78%
Large	13	12	92%	3,882,653	95%
TOTAL	453	299	66%	9,863,335	82%

	Avg LSA	% of 38
	26,492	64%

Pennsylvania has a *lot* of public libraries. Social network participation is above average on both metrics: two-thirds of the libraries and more than four out of five patrons.

The Free Library of Philadelphia is by far the largest library in the state, serving some 1,518,000 people from more than 50 locations. When checked in mid-November 2011, its Facebook page had 6,686 likes (0.4%), and its Twitter account had 4,580 followers (0.3%). Following are a few updates from the active Facebook page and tweets from the *very* active Twitter account:

Tonight! Join the Raven Society at Pub & Kitchen as they celebrate Poe's birthday. Details below: Happy Birthday Poe! Happy Hour Thursday, January 12 at 6:00pm at Pub And Kitchen **7 people like this.**

Congratulations to Walter Dean Myers, named the newest ambassador for young people's literature! **[Link] 13 people like this.**

> **Ruth** way to go!!!!!!!!!!

Oh, the Joy of Books! The Joy of Books **[Link] 45 people like this.**

> **Michael** Keep on reading :o)

Looking for your monthly Dickens fix? Join our Dickens Literary Salons **[Link]**

Boo! Some facts about Friday the 13th [Link]

Always wanted to play an instrument? We can help! Check out these music materials for beginners: [Link]

Lil Wayne can now add author to his resume. Do you enjoy books by non-literary folks? [Link]

RHODE ISLAND

TABLE 7.30

Rhode Island public libraries in social networks

SIZE	LIBS	SN	SN%	SN LSA	SN LSA%
Small	10	7	70%	42,333	72%
Medium	36	26	72%	793,790	77%
Large	1	1	100%	171,909	100%
TOTAL	47	34	72%	1,008,032	80%

Avg LSA	% of 38
26,776	65%

Rhode Island's percentage of public library social network participation is quite high, while the percentage of people served by those libraries is just above average.

Cranston Public Library serves some 80,100 people from five locations. When checked in early November 2011, its Facebook page had 653 likes (0.8%) and its Twitter account, 328 followers (0.4%). Both are reasonably active, with an update or tweet every couple of days. Following are a few updates from January 2012:

Bill and Keith's Excellent Song Title Contest and an appearance on Kids Place Live! [Link] Farm Visits likes this.

UPCOMING WORKSHOP: Online Job Searching with Andrea Eastman, M.S. Career Counselor. In today's world, the Internet is an important resource in the search for work. This workshop will provide tips on searching for jobs online, exploring a variety of sites, both general and industry specific. Participants will need basic computer and Internet experience and an email address before taking the workshop. Location: Central Library For more info and to register call: [#]. **Allison W. likes this.**

Cranston Public Library added 3 new photos to the album eBooks & eReaders Workshops.

SOUTH CAROLINA

TABLE 7.31

South Carolina public libraries in social networks

SIZE	LIBS	SN	SN%	SN LSA	SN LSA%
Small	0	0	0	0	0
Medium	28	17	61%	892,669	71%
Large	14	11	79%	2,209,993	72%
TOTAL	42	28	67%	3,102,662	72%

Avg LSA	% of 38
102,767	248%

South Carolina's relatively small number of public libraries, none of them small or very large, offers a slightly unusual situation: a high percentage of public libraries on social networks but a slightly low percentage of people served by such libraries.

The Spartanburg County Public Libraries serve some 273,000 people from 11 branches and keep in touch with both Twitter (764 followers, 0.3%) and Facebook (1,743 likes, 0.6%). Tweets and updates don't always cover the same ground, and the tweets that do are written to provide a complete (if brief) message. Sample Facebook updates include:

Andy does the Monday minute from the National WWII Museum! Check it out! National WWII Museum **[Link] 2 people like this.**

Jobs Available for Students and Recent Grads Are you a student looking to build up your resume or get some practical experience in your field? Have you just graduated recently, and are looking for some hands-on experience? There are some excellent job-hunting websites devoted specifically for students and recent grads. **[Link] South Carolina State Library likes this.**

Is everyone having a good Shark Week? Tonight (8/5), the Headquarters Library will be showing Soul Surfer at 6:00. **[Wall] 3 people like this.**

Michelle Do u know what its rated

Spartanburg County Public Libraries PG

The library's response to a patron's question in that last update came *two minutes* after the question.

TEXAS

TABLE 7.32

Texas public libraries in social networks

SIZE	LIBS	SN	SN%	SN LSA	SN LSA%
Small	308	81	26%	380,836	28%
Medium	215	113	53%	3,348,011	53%
Large	42	32	76%	13,499,835	87%
TOTAL	565	226	40%	17,228,682	75%

Avg LSA	% of 38
40,793	99%

Texas has a lot of libraries, considerably more than any other state in this survey (but fewer than New York) and three times as many as California, the obvious point of comparison. The percentage of libraries on social networks is on the low side, and the percentage of people served (three out of four) is slightly below average.

Austin Public Library serves 768,000 people from 22 locations and a used bookstore. When checked in late November 2011, its Facebook page had 2,531 likes (0.3%), but its Twitter account had 3,605 followers (0.5%). The Twitter account continues to grow faster than the Facebook page. Here are four tweets from January 2012—and part of one Facebook update that shows effective patron engagement (library name abbreviated to APL and only the first six of 16 comments shown, representing immediate reader's advisory through Facebook; every reader received a useful response):

Family Library Day @ Twin Oaks Branch! Celebrate Texas tree-planting season with crafts & puppet show. 1 pm Sat, Jan 14 **[Link]**

The Teen Book Club at Yarborough will discuss "The Maze Runner" by James Dashner on Thursday, January 12 at 7:00 P.M. **[Link]**

Have a question about our downloadable eBooks/eAudiobooks? Browse our "How Do I?" section or give us a call [#] **[Link]**

@shelbydh78704 Let us know if we can help you find something. We also love suggestions for titles we're missing: **[Link]**

We're bringing our Personal Picks service to Facebook for a day! List three titles you've enjoyed in a comment below, and librarians will suggest a new one.

> **Jean** Love decorating books: better home and gardens, small kitchen solutions, Piet Swimberghe: Vintage style, House Beautiful: small space decorating workshop.

> **Ashli** When Elephants Cry, Unbroken (Laura Hillenbrand), Packing for Mars. Thanks!

> **Tiffany** The Adventures of Sherlock Holmes by Sir Arthur Conan Doyle, The White Mary by Kira Salak, The Lacuna by Barbara Kingsolver

> **Mandy** For my son—Magic Tree House, anything by Matt Christopher and Sideways Stories from Wayside School

> **Becky Anotherdemocrat** I'm waiting impatiently for the 3rd book from Pat Rothfuss, loved Speed of Dark by Elizabeth Moon, and for the great stories, not for the YA-ness: Hunger Games & Sawyer's www trilogy.

[APL] Jean Brandon: The library has some great books on decorating! Here are a few you might like: Anna Starmer's "The Color Scheme Bible: Inspirational Palettes for Designing Home Interiors," Maxwell Gillingham-Ryan's "Apartment Therapy" presents real homes, real people, hundreds of real design solutions, and the recently published "No Place Like Home: Tips & Techniques for Real Family-Friendly Home Design" by Stephen Saint-Onge.

TABLE 7.33

Utah public libraries in social networks

SIZE	LIBS	SN	SN%	SN LSA	SN LSA%
Small	34	16	47%	91,083	59%
Medium	27	18	67%	538,372	66%
Large	6	4	67%	1,245,650	70%
TOTAL	67	38	57%	1,875,105	68%

Avg LSA	% of 38
41,021	99%

While the percentage of Utah's diverse public libraries on social networks is typical at 57%, the percentage of people served is on the low side at 68%, still more than two-thirds.

Garland Public Library serves around 2,100 people, with a reasonably active Facebook account liked in early December 2011 by 180 people—9% of the community. The updates, in this case over a little more than a week, have an appropriate small-town feel:

> Thanks to all the kids (and parents) who came out and rode our Wheat & Beet days float in the parade! We appreciate your support!!

> Congratulations to Torie! She had her baby on Friday at 7pm. Weighed 7 lbs 7 oz. His name is Holden Arthur. **7 people like this.**
>
> **Monica** Congratulations Torie! Sunday at 9:20am

> Stories with Torie (Loriann will be in charge) will be Thurs. Aug 4th at 4:00p.m. at the City Armory. This is the summer reading party for the children. Come prepared to have a blast!!! **Monica likes this.**

> The Adult Summer Reading party is next Wednesday, August 10th at 5:30p.m. If you have read books during the summer, you are invited to attend. We will be making altered books (recipe books) and we will also have an "around the world" Taster's Table. Please bring something to share! Please call the library if you have any questions.

VERMONT

TABLE 7.34

Vermont public libraries in social networks

SIZE	LIBS	SN	SN%	SN LSA	SN LSA%
Small	171	85	50%	248,471	59%
Medium	12	11	92%	196,131	92%
Large	0	0	0	0	0
TOTAL	**183**	**96**	**52%**	**444,602**	**70%**

Avg LSA	% of 38
3,453	8%

Vermont has essentially the same number of public library agencies as California, but California has 60 times as many people. There are no large libraries in Vermont and relatively few medium-sized libraries, so it's not surprising that the state scores slightly low on both social networking metrics. Nevertheless, it's still true that slightly more than half of the libraries are on social networks, serving more than two-thirds of the people.

Greensboro Free Library serves 772 people and has active accounts on both Twitter (11 followers, 1.4%) and Facebook (157 followers, 20%). The tweets and updates are similar, as in these updates from early January 2012:

> "This Day in History"—On this day in 1965, construction is completed on the Gateway Arch, a spectacular 630-foot-high parabola of stainless steel marking the Jefferson National Expansion Memorial on the waterfront of St. Louis, Missouri. **Tamra L. likes this.**

> Don't forget you can search the Greensboro library catalog anytime via the web using this address. Try it out and see what we have! You can even find out whether a book is available to borrow while you're sitting at home. **[Link]**

> The Chili dinner is coming up! Join us on January 20th in Fellowship Hall and take the chill out of winter. Donation only. **2 people like this.**

> New books have arrived! Come check them out and enjoy one on a cold winter day!

VIRGINIA

TABLE 7.35

Virginia public libraries in social networks

SIZE	LIBS	SN	SN%	SN LSA	SN LSA%
Small	9	4	44%	25,249	49%
Medium	62	42	68%	1,639,210	66%
Large	20	17	85%	4,536,785	89%
TOTAL	91	63	69%	6,201,244	81%

Avg LSA	% of 38
84,179	203%

Virginia is considerably higher than average on percentage of public libraries on social networks and just above average on patrons served by those libraries.

Bristol Public Library serves 42,000 people from two locations. When checked in early November 2011, its Twitter account had 689 followers (1.6%), and its Facebook page had 1,426 likes (3.4%). Both accounts are very active with generally identical content. Some updates from early January 2012 include:

FREE Customer Service Workshop—Tuesday, March 6 at 10:00am at Bristol Public Library.

FREE Business Basics Workshop—Tuesday, February 7 at 9:30am at Bristol Public Library.

"It may not be the Garden of Eden but you still shouldn't eat the apples." Check this out! Garden Spells by Sarah Addison Allen **2 people like this.**

   Jeanne Garden Spells is one of my all time favorite books!

FREE Credit Counseling Workshop—at Bristol Public Library. **Burger Bar likes this.**

WASHINGTON

TABLE 7.36

Washington public libraries in social networks

SIZE	LIBS	SN	SN%	SN LSA	SN LSA%
Small	27	13	48%	64,790	72%
Medium	21	12	57%	422,095	63%
Large	15	15	100%	5,780,850	100%
TOTAL	63	40	63%	6,267,735	96%

Avg LSA	% of 38
103,877	251%

One figure jumps out in Washington's picture: 96%. Nearly all Washington residents are served by libraries on social networks, even though slightly less than two-thirds of the libraries are on such networks.

The Denny Ashby Library in Pomeroy isn't one of Washington's largest, serving some 2,000 people, and when checked in early December 2011, more than 9% of the community, 211 in all, liked the library's active Facebook account. Examples from earlier in the year include:

> C.J. Box will be visiting the Asotin County Library in November and our Friends of the Library are planning to fill a community van full of his readers to join in the conversation. More information coming soon! Review: C.J. Box delivers suspenseful wilderness thriller with 'Back of Beyond' [Link] Katy McK. likes this.

> How does one move a family of 999 young frogs? Kids Book Review: Review: *999 Tadpoles Find a New Home* [Link] Russell C. likes this.

> "Take a good hard look at who you are and what you have . . . and then use it." Book review: "A Good Hard Look" by Ann Napolitano [Link]

> Take a look at new material recently added to the Garfield County Heritage digital collection through the library's 2010–2011 project grant from the Washington State Library. (Please pass along any needed corrections/ further identifications you are able to provide!) [Link] Angie likes this.

> **Denny Ashby Library** See the rest of this year's grant material here: [Link]

WISCONSIN

TABLE 7.37

Wisconsin public libraries in social networks

SIZE	LIBS	SN	SN%	SN LSA	SN LSA%
Small	260	139	53%	614,982	62%
Medium	114	84	74%	2,329,447	76%
Large	7	7	100%	1,615,003	100%
TOTAL	381	230	60%	4,559,432	80%

Avg LSA	% of 38
14,950	36%

Social network participation for Wisconsin's varied public libraries is a little more than average for libraries and essentially average for people, with four out of five covered by participating libraries.

LaValle Public Library serves a community of 600 people, but it manages to be open five days a week and operate both a Facebook page and a Twitter account. When checked in mid-November 2011, the library had 47 Twitter followers (8%) and Facebook 67 likes (11%). The updates may be frequent enough for this size library. Following are examples from Twitter during two weeks in mid-December (Facebook updates are similar):

> In the Loop . . . with the Friends of the La Valle Library When I was 10 years old, I had an amazing job. I worked . . . [Link]

> @madisonlibrary We sure will enjoy our visit from Santa! Hope your move is going well! Wishing you all the best from LaValle!

> On the verge of getting movie license. Perhaps we'll squeeze in "Meet Me in St. Louis" before XMas time? That would simply make the season.

> HO HO HO!! SANTA IS COMING TO LA VALLE LIBRARY! Saturday, December 10th from 10:00am–Noon (TD)

WYOMING

TABLE 7.38

Wyoming public libraries in social networks

SIZE	LIBS	SN	SN%	SN LSA	SN LSA%
Small	8	4	50%	26,007	48%
Medium	15	13	87%	452,300	92%
Large	0	0	0	0	0
TOTAL	23	17	74%	478,307	88%

Avg LSA	% of 38
23,664	57%

Since Wyoming has fewer than 600,000 people in all, it's hardly surprising that it has no large libraries and relatively few library systems in all. The libraries are considerably more active in social networks than average, with nearly three-quarters of public libraries involved, serving nearly nine out of 10 people.

When checked in early December 2011, Natrona County Public Library was one of two Wyoming libraries with both Twitter and Facebook accounts (the only one with a Twitter account when I first checked in August 2011). The library serves some 75,000 people in and around Casper from four locations. The Twitter account had 103 followers (0.1%) and only occasional tweets when checked in mid-January 2012 (none since mid-November 2011). The Facebook page has 996 likes (1.3%), the most of any Wyoming public library, and is fairly active. Following are three updates from August 2011:

> Saturday is the LAST DAY to turn in all summer reading logs for kids, teens and adults. Way to read! Good luck in the grand prize drawings! **4 people like this.**

> Have you checked out an eBook yet? Since July 1st, we've checked out 363 titles! I'm reading Betty White's newest book "If You Ask Me (and of course you won't)" **Rebecca likes this.**

>> **Rebecca** Not yet, but I reallly want a Nook Color for my birthday :)

>> **Natrona County Public Library** I have the purple Kobo touch—I had the regular kobo and liked it but this touch is wonderful!! Kate

> Here's the perfect book for a bad day—Other People's Rejection Letters: 150 Letters You're Happy You Didn't Get. Did you know Jimi Hendrix was kicked out of the Army? That, at one time, women were not allowed to be cartoonists at Disney? Take a look at these original rejection letters and feel better about your day. **[Link] 3 people like this.**

CHAPTER 8

....

THE CHANGING PICTURE AND CLOSING THOUGHTS

BY NOW YOU should have a sense of the state of public libraries on social networks in late fall 2011, at least for 38 states. But that's a rolling snapshot, and if there's one legitimate truism about social networks it is that the scene is always changing. When I began work on this book, Google+ didn't exist—and it became usable for libraries only as I was finishing the 38-state sweep. If the picture was studied again in late 2013, I'd venture a guess that hundreds of public libraries will have Google+ pages, and this will be just one example of change.

This chapter looks at changes over the course of four months—17 weeks, give or take two days—in social network activity in public libraries within 25 states, including more than half of the U.S. population but fewer than one-third of the public libraries (2,406 in all). For those 2,406 libraries, I began checking library websites and taking information on Twitter and Facebook on July 25, 2011, and concluded the sweep on August 22, 2011. I went back to the libraries beginning November 25, 2011, working in the same order as the original survey and concluding on December 20, 2011. The time lag between first check and second check was never fewer than 119 days and never more than 123 days.

One caveat on changes reported here: To some extent, actual changes in library activity can be masked by changes in findability. I used slightly more extensive and regular techniques in the late fall sweep, so I'd expect that factor to mostly mean the inclusion of some new Facebook pages and Twitter accounts that weren't new but that I didn't previously find. Changes in Google's algorithms could also mean that some previously findable libraries and accounts weren't findable the second time around (or vice versa).

There's another small caveat: My guidelines for inclusion in the summer were tighter than in the fall. In the summer, a library had to have at least one like and at least one update for a Facebook page to be included and at least one follower and one tweet for a Twitter account to be included. In the fall, as long as it was clear that the page or account was under a library's control, I counted empty accounts—those with no likes or updates and those with no followers or tweets. That's a small factor, less than 3 percent of the social network accounts.

I've included my comments throughout these chapters, but I'll add a few closing thoughts after a quick look at changes over the four months from August to December 2011.

· The States ·

States included in the first sweep are Alaska, Arizona, California, Colorado, Connecticut, Florida, Georgia, Idaho, Kentucky, Louisiana, Maryland, Minnesota, Mississippi, Missouri, Montana, Nevada, New Jersey, New Mexico, North Carolina, Oklahoma, Oregon, South Carolina, Utah, Washington, and Wyoming. In all, libraries in those states serve just under 166 million people—more than half of the country.

FACEBOOK CHANGES

In the summer of 2011, I found 1,139 Facebook pages among the 2,406 libraries, or 47% of the libraries. In the fall, I found 1,267 Facebook pages (and groups and accounts), or 53% of the libraries.

Does that mean 128 libraries added Facebook pages during those four months? Not necessarily. When I compared the old and new situations for each library, I found 1,083 continuing pages, 53 pages that I could no longer find, and 184 new pages.

Of the so-called new pages, I'm reasonably confident that at least 50 of them are either new or weren't included earlier because they had no activity. These are pages with no updates at all or fewer than four. I'm inclined to believe that most of the other pages are also legitimately new; it certainly wouldn't be surprising for 8% of the libraries to start Facebook pages over a four-month period.

CHANGES IN LIKES

Looking at the 1,083 Facebook pages I could locate in both sweeps, the total number of likes increased by 52,800, from some 431,000 to some 484,000, for a gain of 12%. The average gain was 49 new likes; the median, 21.

Behind those overall numbers are some interesting variations. Two libraries added more than 2,500 likes each; 11 added between 500 and 999 (none added 1,000 to 2,499); 24 more added 250 to 499 likes; and 84 added 100 to 249 likes. On the other hand, 17 had no net change at all; 13 lost from one to five likes during the period; and 14 lost significant numbers of likes during the period. For six of those 14, the explanation seems simple enough: The page had never had actual updates or the page was essentially abandoned. In at least one case that I checked, it appears that the library abandoned one Facebook page (or old group) and started a new one that hasn't yet gotten lots of likes. It's fair to say that most library Facebook pages continue to add likes.

Percentage changes in likes are probably more meaningful than raw counts. Following are some items to note:

- Eleven library Facebook pages had gains of 700 to 8,000%, which translates to adding anywhere from seven to 106 likes, since none of these pages had more than six likes in the first sweep and eight of the 11 had one like each.

- Likes more than doubled for another 30 library Facebook pages over the four-month interval, including some pages with hundreds or even thousands of likes in summer 2011. For example, Shreve Memorial Library in Louisiana went from 434 likes on August 9, 2011, to 2,983 on December 8, 2011, and Kenton County Public Library in Kentucky went from 2,456 likes on August 17 to 6,065 likes on December 17. I find it impressive that 41 libraries in all—4% of the libraries with ongoing Facebook pages—more than doubled their audience in a relatively short period.
- Another 37 libraries gained at least 50% in Facebook likes, and 130 more gained at least 25%.
- Most of the rest had significant but less major gains. Forty-four library Facebook pages had essentially the same size audience (gaining 1%, showing no change, or losing 1% or 2%), six showed mild declines (–3% to –11%, but only one of those was an actual decline of more than four likes), and 15 showed significant declines, including two libraries—each of which had a single post over the entire life of the Facebook page—that lost all their likes. (The group showing major losses includes another library with no Facebook updates, another with only one, and one with three.)
- Overall, 1,017 of the library Facebook pages—94% of them—picked up a significant number of likes during the four-month period.

· Twitter Changes ·

In the summer sweep, I found a total of 369 Twitter accounts. In the fall update, I found 487—just one out of five libraries, but a considerable gain. A little of this may be findability, but I believe it was mostly accounts established within the four months. (Fourteen Twitter accounts either disappeared or became unfindable, so the actual number of new accounts, or accounts that finally started tweeting and gained followers, was 133, an increase of 36% over four months. I don't find that improbable.)

Of the 14 defunct, disappeared, or newly unfindable Twitter accounts, eight had fewer than 100 tweets when checked in the summer of 2011 and only two had more than 40 followers.

CHANGES IN FOLLOWERS

Looking at 353 Twitter accounts that were findable (and had at least one follower) in both summer and fall, the total followers increased from just over 119,000 to just under 139,000. Adding up all the changes in followers yielded a gain of just over 19,500, but only one library showed a significant loss of followers, and that appears to be a case where one Twitter account was abandoned and another begun because the library shows some 2,000 fewer total tweets in late fall than it did in summer.

While no library gained more than 700 followers in four months, four gained more than 500, another 11 gained more than 250, and 45 more gained more than 100 followers. Eleven libraries either stayed constant or lost one follower, and five others (in addition to the one anomaly already noted) lost three to seven followers.

Looking at percentage changes, six libraries at least tripled the number of Twitter followers over four months, but only two of those had 10 or more followers in the summer (those two went from 95 to 264 followers and 48 to 101 followers, respectively). Eighteen additional libraries more than doubled their number of followers, but here again only two of the 18 had more than 23 followers in the summer, and those two had 32 and 43 followers (growing to 82 and 90), respectively.

Twenty-five library Twitter accounts gained more than 50% (but less than 100%) in followers over four months, including several with hundreds of followers. Seventy libraries gained between one-quarter and one-half in followers over three months. That's 129 libraries in all with quite substantial gains in followers over four months, or slightly more than a third of all the Twitter accounts. Another 148 gained from 10 to 24%; in other words, three-quarters of the continuing accounts had significant growth over four months. As before, 17 (5%) either stayed steady or lost ground.

TWEET FREQUENCY

Thanks to Twitter's general transparency (except for one library account that protects tweets unless you're a follower), it was also possible to determine exactly how frequently libraries tweeted during the four-month period.

Looking at total tweets revealed two other anomalous accounts. One very active account with more than 1,500 followers and a healthy gain in followers over four months somehow had more than 1,300 *fewer* total tweets in late fall 2011 than in the summer. Another library had a Twitter account with three followers and two total tweets in the summer and an account with three followers and *no* total tweets in the fall. Ignoring those anomalies and looking at 350 Twitter accounts, the total number of tweets grew from 193,075 when checked in the summer to 235,106 when checked in late fall: more than 42,000 tweets, or an average of 120 per account or, rather neatly, 30 per month or one per day.

Nice as it is to simply say that the average library Twitter account had one tweet per day in late 2011, that's no more likely to be meaningful than is any other average. The median, a slightly more meaningful figure, is half that: 15.6 per month, or one tweet every other day. In other words, half the libraries tweeted at least once every other day, and half tweeted less often. That second half includes 10 accounts with no tweets at all over the four-month period.

Following are some data points on tweeting activity:

- The most frequent tweeter, Missoula Public Library in Montana, averaged 341 tweets per month, or about 11 per day. Checked again as I was writing this chapter in February 2012, that account is indeed high frequency (11 tweets in the last 24 hours on a holiday; another 11 yesterday, a Sunday; and another 10 on the day before that) with primarily tweets written as such, lots of retweets, and a fair amount of conversation. More than 700 people follow those tweets, which I have no doubt they enjoy.
- Three other libraries averaged more than 200 tweets per month, or six per day; another 19 averaged more than 93 tweets per month, or three per day. Adding 26 more libraries with at least two tweets per day gives us a total of 49 library Twitter accounts—14% of the accounts considered here—that averaged two or more tweets per day.
- Fifty-five more libraries averaged at least one tweet a day—that makes 104, or 30% of the total.
- Seventy-one more (20%) averaged at least a tweet every other day.

- Dropping below the median, 44 libraries averaged a tweet every third day, 32 averaged a tweet every fourth day, and 45 averaged a tweet per week. In all, 296 (85%) tweeted at least weekly.
- Infrequent tweeters included 21 averaging two to four tweets per month, 10 averaging a tweet per month, and 13 averaging less than a tweet per month but with some tweets during the four months. In all, that's 44 libraries (13%) with very few tweets in addition to the 10 libraries with none at all.

What about the 10 wholly inactive libraries? Most, but not all, had never been very active or had many followers. There are always exceptions, however, as one library managed to add 22 followers, for a 13% gain, over four months and went from 74 total tweets to . . . 74 total tweets. At least those followers weren't overloaded!

· Closing Thoughts ·

It would be easy enough to paint a picture of social networking as a failure for public libraries. Few of them reach even 10% of their potential patrons. Overall, relatively few posts get comments at all, and the number of actual conversations taking place on library accounts is fairly low. Certainly, no public library in the 38 states surveyed reached as many people via social networks as, say, Ashton Kutcher (@aplusk, more than 14.3 million followers) or McDonald's (more than 1.2 million followers).

But those are, I believe, inappropriate measures of success. If you want to go there, the fact is that America's public libraries had *more* followers in late 2011 than McDonald's (298,000 within the 38 surveyed states compared to McDonald's 247,000)—and that's a meaningless bit of information.

This book notes failures, but deliberately avoids naming them. Libraries fail with Twitter or Facebook when they stop posting entirely, when they don't respond to patron requests and comments, or when they allow spam to remain on the library's wall. I believe libraries hamper their success when they fail to make their social network accounts down-to-earth and human. Maybe large libraries should have initialed or signed posts, maybe not—but it almost always helps to have updates and, especially, tweets appear in a recognizably casual form that hasn't been approved rather than a bland, lifeless, corporate neutrality.

I believe it also helps Twitter accounts a *lot* to prepare tweets separately from Facebook updates, so the tweets are meaningful even before you get to the shortened link.

Most libraries that continue to participate in social networks are succeeding. The success is modest in most cases. It could be better in the vast majority of cases. I hope this book will help in this regard.

Should every library have a Twitter account? Of course not, any more than every library should have a dedicated teen room. As with blogs, I believe that the case for Facebook pages and Twitter accounts is straightforward: Any library can *potentially* benefit from having one—but for many libraries, that potential comes at too high a cost in time and attention. In some cases, the return isn't worth the investment when compared to other opportunities and when balanced against available time.

I've deliberately chosen a wide range of examples of library Facebook and Twitter accounts in action. A few of these may be the ones you always hear about, but most of them aren't. Quite a few of them are much more successful than average, but not all.

I'd marked another two dozen libraries as having particularly interesting Facebook or Twitter usage, in addition to the 80-odd libraries used as examples in this book. That includes libraries that feature local history in their updates, libraries coping with local emergencies and serving as community lifelines, Facebook pages with fairly lengthy updates (and ones where the Facebook updates are no longer than Twitter's 140-word limit), libraries unafraid to become involved in controversies (especially when those controversies involve library funding), writers with refreshingly honest comments and pages with distinctly personal styles, and more. There are many ways to succeed in social networking, most of which have much to do with the library staff's involvement with and sense of the community. I found it refreshing and enlightening—and only occasionally disappointing—to read tweet streams and walls from more than 3,000 public libraries.

It would be interesting and, I believe, useful to see how public library use of social networks changes over time. This book is based on a rolling snapshot from fall 2011 and, in this chapter, on changes from an earlier, smaller snapshot in summer 2011.

What will the scene be like in fall 2013? I can offer some guesses:

- There will be quite a few more public library Twitter accounts, probably several hundred more—and a few (or a few dozen) existing accounts will wither away or disappear entirely.
- There will be more public library Facebook pages, but certainly not as many more as Twitter in terms of percentage growth. I wonder whether the saturation point for realistic Facebook pages might be around two-thirds of libraries?
- There will be hundreds but probably not thousands of Google+ pages.
- There may be a few dozen remaining MySpace icons on public library pages, but I wonder whether most of those won't lead to deserted or entirely defunct pages.

Those are guesses. I'd love to know the actual numbers, but that's a major project.

In the meantime, thousands of libraries reach more than a million people through social network accounts—and that's a good thing.

APPENDIX
Surveying the Libraries

WHEN THIS PROJECT began, I planned to check all the libraries in California and at least one other state in order to provide a small but plausible cross-section of America's public libraries. California is my own state, and it represents some 18% of the U.S. population and has a reasonable number of library agencies that includes libraries and systems large and small, urban and rural, wealthy and poor. I planned to check at least one other state because California also isn't typical—if there is such a thing as "typical" when it comes to public libraries. As work progressed, the sample size grew substantially.

The best previous study of this sort that I'm aware of was Zeth Lietzau and Jamie Helgren's *U.S. Public Libraries and the Use of Web Technologies, 2010*, published in April 2011 by Colorado's Library Research Service (LRS) and freely available at www.lrs.org/documents/web20/Web Tech2010_CloserLookReport_Final.pdf. That study, which continued a baseline LRS study done in 2008, included 125 libraries from each of four service population groups and added all of the largest public library systems (those serving more than 500,000 people) and, separately, all 114 of Colorado's public libraries. The need to include libraries of different sizes was clear to those involved in the LRS study: "Public libraries of different sizes have vastly different characteristics in terms of inputs and usage, and these differences no doubt appear in the realm of web technology usage as well."[1]

The LRS study found that 80% of the largest libraries had Facebook accounts in 2010, as did 58% of those serving 100,000 to 499,999, 56% of those serving 25,000 to 99,999, 44% of those serving 10,000 to 24,999, and 18% of those serving fewer than 10,000 people. (The Twitter percentages were, respectively, 68%, 38%, 22%, 15%, and 3%.) That represents enormous growth from 2008, when the figures were 11%, 5%, 1%, 3%, and 1%, respectively. It's not entirely clear how these determinations were made (the publication says LRS "examined the websites" of the public libraries, which as you'll see later in this appendix can result in substantially undercounting Facebook presence). The LRS study offered a first-rate look at use of a number of contemporary technologies in a reasonably large cross-section of public libraries, and it helped encourage me to do a larger (but also more focused) study.

As the summer progressed, I checked all the public libraries in 25 states—half of the United States with 54% of the nation's population. It was a broadly representative reflection of the nation's public libraries, although clearly biased toward larger libraries. Let's look at the study in more detail. (Most of the next section first appeared in slightly different form in the October 2011 *Cites & Insights*, available at http://citesandinsights.info/civ11i9.pdf.)

SAMPLING LIBRARY WEBSITES

I looked at a lot of public library websites between July 26, 2011, and August 22, 2011. I would say 2,406 of them, but that's not entirely accurate. I looked for public library websites for 2,406 libraries and library agencies (henceforth, just libraries, or basically agencies that report statistics to their state library and IMLS), but in 176 cases—7.3%—I didn't find sites I considered to be legitimate library websites.

The Sample

The sample of public library websites is intended to be a reasonable cross-section of America's public libraries. What began with California and one other state grew to be California and five other states, deliberately stratified by population: New Jersey, Minnesota, Mississippi, Idaho, and Wyoming. Those are the first, 11th, 21st, 31st, 39th, and 50th most populous states in 2010. Why the 39th most populous and not the 40th or 41st? Hawaii is the 40th most populous state, but it's entirely served by branches of one public library and seemed too atypical to be a good inclusion. Maine is 41st, and with 269 reporting libraries for a relatively small state, it felt like too much of a burden at the time. (Idaho, by comparison, has 104 libraries.)

After finishing Wyoming on August 4, 2011, I decided to enlarge the sample further, looking for states that met two criteria:

- The state library had to have a downloadable spreadsheet or table with library names and legal service areas. (Twelve states do not appear to have such spreadsheets, and I cheated in one or two cases, retyping data from PDF reports.)
- The number of libraries needed to be "reasonable"—I omitted states with huge numbers of libraries.

That filter added Florida, Washington, Arizona, South Carolina, Louisiana, Utah, New Mexico, Montana, Alaska, Georgia, North Carolina, Missouri, Maryland, Nevada, Oklahoma, Colorado, Kentucky, and Oregon. At that point, I had 24 states and added Connecticut, with a relatively large number of libraries for its population, to make it 25.

While this survey includes half of the states, it does *not* include half of the libraries. As defined by state agencies and reported to the Institute of Museum and Library Services—or in this case as used in the latest HAPLR figures, since those include a useful breakdown of libraries by population served—there were just under 9,200 public libraries, so the survey includes only 26% of the libraries. On the other hand, the libraries surveyed serve a total of more than 165 million people, more than half the nation's total (even including double counting, which happens in a few cases).

The list of states is very strong in the Old West and Far West, fairly strong in the South, and weak in New England and the Midwest. I believe it's a reasonably good cross-section of large, small, urban, and rural states. But the more I looked at it, the more I wondered whether even this large sample was good enough.

The Bias

The bias is, as noted, deliberate: except for New Jersey, studied before I realized there was a problem, it's biased toward states with relatively few reporting libraries for their size, which allowed me to include quite a few states while still being able to do the survey in a reasonable amount of time. (For example, California has 181 libraries serving more than 37 million people, while Texas has 561 serving 25 million and Massachusetts has 370 serving 6.5 million.)

I'll point to Wyoming, New Mexico, Montana, and Alaska, at the very least, to suggest that it would be inappropriate to accuse me of ignoring smaller and rural libraries. However, it's true that the bias toward fewer reporting libraries results in an oversampling of larger libraries and an undersampling of smaller ones.

How serious is that bias? If you use one common dividing line between larger ("urban") and smaller ("rural") libraries—25,000 as a service area population—my sample includes nearly 62% of smaller libraries, but nearly 78% of U.S. public libraries fall into the smaller categories.

Table A.1 shows how this works out using HAPLR population divisions (and most recent numbers) as a basis.

TABLE A.1

Twenty-five-state survey compared to HAPLR, by size of libraries

LSA	HAPLR	LSN	LSN%	L OF H	BIAS
<1,000	1,072	174	7.23%	16.23%	−38.04%
1–2.4K	1,524	233	9.68%	15.29%	−41.64%
2.5–4.9K	1,310	232	9.64%	17.71%	−32.40%
5–9K	1,483	330	13.72%	22.25%	−15.06%
10–24K	1,764	520	21.61%	29.48%	12.52%
25–49K	952	325	13.51%	34.14%	30.31%
50–99K	556	244	10.14%	43.88%	67.51%
100–249K	335	214	8.89%	63.88%	143.84%
250–499K	104	72	2.99%	69.23%	164.26%
500,000+	84	62	2.58%	73.81%	181.74%
TOTAL	9,184	2,406		26.20%	
Rural	7,153	1,489	61.89%	20.82%	−20.54%
Urban	2,031	917	38.11%	45.15%	72.34%
Small	5,389	969	40.27%	17.98%	−31.36%
Medium	3,272	1,089	45.26%	33.28%	27.04%
Large	523	348	14.46%	66.54%	153.99%

Interpreting table A.1 in words, the 25-state survey includes about two-thirds of large libraries (those serving at least 100,000 people), about one-third of medium-sized libraries (those serving 10,000 to 99,999 people), and about one-sixth of small libraries (those serving fewer than 10,000 people). It's still a broader survey than any I'm aware of that looks at social network participation.

Methodology

I downloaded library names (or city or county names, if that's what the state library uses) and legal service area (LSA) populations for the libraries in these states to a single master spreadsheet. I then used Bing to find each library's website and followed links from the websites. If I couldn't find a website or there was no Facebook link, I looked for a Facebook page in the next 15 to 25 results.

When, or if, I found a Facebook page, I noted the number of likes, copied the most recent five updates, and determined the number of months covered by the most recent 20 Facebook updates (or in some cases *all* of the library's updates). For Twitter accounts, I noted numbers of followers, following, and tweets; copied the five most recent tweets; and noted the number of months covered by the most recent 20 tweets. I added the date of the test, since I'd already decided to do a follow-up, and later, I looked at the five posts and tweets for signs of interactivity and for the currency of the most recent post or tweet.

Being Realistic

If I was trying to prove something about public library websites across the nation, this sample would be inadequate—and frankly, I believe any sample short of 100% is likely to be inadequate. Public libraries are wildly heterogeneous. Even within my biased survey, there are 17 libraries with LSA populations of fewer than 100 people each (that's 100, not a mistyped 1,000) and 19 with LSAs of more than one million people each. Consider the extreme. The largest library system in these 25 states, Los Angeles Public Library, has an LSA of 4.095 million people. To achieve that number of people starting with the smallest library takes 997 libraries—every library serving 10,000 or fewer, and 26 of those serving more than 10,000. If you love classic rock, you'll find it interesting that the cutoff library is Winslow, Arizona.

I'm not trying to prove anything about library websites as a whole. I'm looking at how a large sampling of public libraries do or don't use two key social networks. If anything, generalizing from the 25 states studied probably overstates the use of social networks, as very small libraries are considerably less likely to be on Twitter or Facebook than very large libraries.

The Missing 176

It might be worth breaking down the missing 176—the libraries where I couldn't find a proper home page at all. You may not be surprised to learn that none of them is in the top three population categories—that is, none serves at least 100,000 people. Two are in the 50,000–99,999 group (which surprises me). Seven are in the 25,000–49,999 group. Eighteen libraries where I couldn't find websites serve 10,000 to 24,999 people, 16 serve 5,000 to 9,999, and 23 serve 2,500 to 4,999. Finally, 34 serve 1,000 to 2,499 people, and 76 serve fewer than 1,000 people (including 14 serving fewer than 100).

A pessimist would note that more than 40% of the smallest libraries and more than 14% of libraries serving 1,000 to 2,499 people didn't have websites that I could find. An optimist would note that 60% of the smallest libraries and more than 85% of the next smallest *did* have findable websites—as did nearly 90% of those serving 2,500 to 4,999 people and more than 95% of any larger category. All things considered, I believe those are great numbers, and in some states they say a lot about initiatives that spread basic library website templates throughout a state or region, such as the one seemingly named for a *Price Is Right* game. (Yes, I do mean Plinkit.)

The Second Pass

As I completed that pass of 2,406 libraries in 25 states, I was in contact with Susan Mark, statistics librarian at the Wyoming State Library. She had her own list of Facebook-using libraries among Wyoming's compact population (23 library systems)—and it didn't match mine, not by a long shot. I had only half as many Facebook users as she did.

After some back and forth, I concluded that I was missing a few libraries that use Facebook but do *not* have an obvious link to the Facebook page on their home pages. Rechecking the Wyoming libraries where I'd come up empty the first time around, but using Google and finding "Facebook" within the first 100 results (Google because, although I was getting better results for library websites from Bing, Bing wouldn't show more than 50 results per page, where Google would show 100), I found all but one of the pages Susan Mark was aware of (and that one was explainable for other reasons).

I tried another 100 libraries in other states where I hadn't found Facebook pages the first time around, again using Google and find-on-this-page in Firefox. The results convinced me to do a second pass of the roughly 1,500 libraries that didn't show a Facebook or Twitter account on the first pass. That second pass, done in the first two weeks of September 2011, yielded another 296 library Facebook pages that were there during the original survey—in addition to hundreds of Community Pages that didn't have status updates. The numbers in this book reflect both the first and second passes, and I'm grateful to Susan Mark for indirectly alerting me to this problem. (I also found half a dozen pages established after I'd first looked; those Facebook accounts will show up as part of the follow-up survey.)

Another Expansion

I started work on the manuscript itself in early fall 2011, and the more I worked, the more I became uneasy with even the very large sample I'd chosen. So I decided to expand it a little, as time allowed, one state at a time.

First, I downloaded the spreadsheets from all the remaining states where I could *find* spreadsheets and copied the library-name and LSA columns to a new combined spreadsheet. I found spreadsheets for 13 of the 25 remaining states. I looked at available IMLS data for the remaining 12. Without a copy of Access or more programming than I was ready to do at the time (I spent five decades as a programmer/analyst; I've done my time), I could not find a way to extract the library names and LSA figures for those states. (In more recent attempts, Excel succeeded at opening the Access databases.)

Then, I started filling in other columns on the new spreadsheet, one state at a time, figuring I'd stop when the labor appeared to outweigh the benefits (and deliberately moving states with a large number of libraries—Massachusetts, Pennsylvania, Texas, and Wisconsin—to the bottom of the spreadsheet).

Methodology

Following is the process I used for this pass:

- I searched for the library using the name as provided in the spreadsheet, adding the state name and "Library" or "County Library" or "Public Library" when needed and in some cases normalizing the forms used in the state library's spreadsheet slightly. These searches were done using Google because it can be set to return 100 results at a time, even though I find that Bing generally yields better results.

- If I found a library website, I looked on the home page for Facebook and Twitter links—either icons or text notes. I went beyond the home page if there was clear evidence of a "Social Networks" or "Social Media" tab or link.
- For each link found that actually resulted in a Facebook page or group or a Twitter page, I noted "w" (for "website") in an appropriate column. Then I noted relevant figures for the page itself (see below).
- If I didn't find a link, I searched for "facebook" or "twitter" within the results page. If I could find the library's page, I noted "g" (for "Google") in the appropriate column and went on to record relevant figures. If I could find community or other informational Facebook pages, but none that appeared to be library controlled, I noted "i" (for "informational") in the Facebook location column.
- If I didn't find Facebook or Twitter pages in Google, I searched for the library name directly within my Facebook or Twitter account. This was rarely useful, but it yielded results just often enough to keep doing it. If I found a page this way, I recorded "f" or "t" (for "Facebook" or "Twitter," respectively) and went on to note relevant figures.
- Relevant figures for Facebook pages included number of likes (or friends or group members). Currency bucket for most recent update included "d" (last 24 hours), "e" (last seven days), "f" (last 14 days), "m" (last month—that is, later than this day on the previous month), "q" (last quarter—that is, later than this day three months earlier), "s" (last six months—later than this day six months earlier), "y" (last year—later than this day in the previous year), or "z" (more than a year old). Currency bucket for the fifth most recent update was "z" if there were fewer than five updates, with a note in the rightmost comment column, "FB1" through "FB4." (If there were no updates from the library at all, I noted "FB0" but left the two buckets blank.) Interactivity notes included "y" if I saw at least one comment that wasn't spam or from a librarian within the most recent 20 or 30 posts; "1" if I saw at least one post-level like but no other comments; and "s" if I saw only spam comments (mostly either work-at-home pitches or pitches from AuthorHouse authors for their books).
- Relevant figures for Twitter pages included number of followers, number of follows, and number of tweets. The same currency buckets were used as for Facebook, as well as the same interactivity notes, but based on tweets starting with "@" or marked as retweets within the first 20 or so tweets.

RESULTS

This process proved to be fast enough that I was able to add all 13 states, resulting in an overall database of 38 states and 5,958 libraries, which was just under two-thirds of all libraries in the United States. The set of 38 states is much more regionally balanced than the 25-state set.

I used this same process to update results for the first 25 states, doing so almost precisely four months after the first check of each library. (The new check was never more than three days before or two days after the four-month interval.) The updated results were used throughout this book, and since I could compare actual tweet totals for libraries using Twitter, I could add some verifiable frequency-of-tweets information (see chapter 8).

The results appear in this book, but let's compare my findings in late 2011 to the LRS findings from 2010.

- **Libraries serving fewer than 10,000 potential patrons (HAPLR categories 0–3, my "small" cluster):** LRS looked at 125 libraries, finding 18% on Facebook and 3% on Twitter. I looked at 3,139 libraries and found just under 42% on Facebook and 5% on Twitter. Here I'm almost certain that it's not just a question of one year's growth.
- **Libraries serving 10,000 to 24,999 (HAPLR category 4):** LRS looked at 125 libraries, finding 44% on Facebook and 15% on Twitter. I looked at 1,235 libraries, finding 63% on Facebook and 18% on Twitter.
- **Libraries serving 25,000 to 99,999 (HAPLR categories 5 and 6):** LRS looked at 125 libraries, finding 56% on Facebook, 22% on Twitter. I looked at 1,104 libraries, finding 69% on Facebook, 29% on Twitter.
- **Libraries serving 100,000 to 499,999 (HAPLR categories 7 and 8):** LRS looked at 125 libraries, finding 58% on Facebook, 38% on Twitter. I looked at 402 libraries, finding 74% on Facebook, 48% on Twitter.
- **Libraries serving 500,000 and up (HAPLR category 9):** LRS looked at all 84 libraries, finding 80% on Facebook, 68% on Twitter. I looked at 78 of the 84 libraries, finding 90% on Facebook, 78% on Twitter.

If there's a lesson here, it's that American libraries really are wildly heterogeneous, such that any sample much smaller than 100% may not be representative. I don't even project my 38-state sample to the nation as a whole, although I'd guess it's not too far off the money.

NOTE

1. Zeth Lietzau and Jamie Helgren, *U.S. Public Libraries and the Use of Web Technologies, 2010* (Denver: Library Research Service, 2011), 7, www.lrs.org/documents/web20/WebTech2010_CloserLookReport_Final.pdf.

Index